JOHN BULL'S FAMOUS CIRCUS

The number of humorous political postcards produced during the present 'troubles' is low, mainly because of the depth of the tragedy which has scarred a generation, but even in the most adverse circumstances humour has a part to play in how people perceive their situation. The caption on the reverse side of this card (published in March 1985) reads: Afternoon Class in Motor Maintenance: Week 3 'The Exhaust System'.

John Bull's

Famous Circus

Ulster History
through the Postcard
1905~1985

John Killen

The O'Brien Press

First published 1985 by The O'Brien Press Ltd.,
20 Victoria Road, Dublin 6.

© copyright reserved

British Library Cataloguing in Publication Data
Killen, John
John Bull's famous circus
1. Postal cards—Northern Ireland
2. Northern Ireland—Politics and government—
Pictorial and government—Pictorial works
I. Title
769'.499416082   DA990.04

ISBN 0-86278-039-X

10 9 8 7 6 5 4 3 2 1

Jacket and book design: Michael O'Brien
Planning & origination: Debby Bell & Colin McDonald
Typesetting: Redsetter Ltd.
Printing: Irish Elsevier Printers, Shannon
Binding: Library Bindings

CONTENTS

SEARCHING FOR ARMS IN ULSTER.

They're howldin' on to Murphy, who thinks he's found a gun,
While O'Flanigan is divin' through a winda' at the run,
And Constable O'Hooligan inspects the chimney pot ;
But divil a wan av all av them a popgun, sure, has got.

To Emma, Jonathan, Stephen and Orla

but especially

to Marian

INTRODUCTION

The idea for this book came from the interest generated by an exhibition of Ulster postcards held in the Linen Hall Library in June 1979. Many themes were portrayed in the exhibition but it was obvious that special interest centred on the political postcards. The general public was intrigued by these mementos of a bygone era, which had become important historical source material.

Much information can be gleaned from the cards shown here, but as far as possible I have sought to let them tell their own story; they are an ideal instrument for illustrating the history and politics of a specific time and place. Text, accordingly, has been kept to a minimum, and there has been no attempt to indulge in political analysis – readers must make their own interpretation of what they see.

Many people and institutions have been unfailingly kind and helpful to me in my researches. Whole collections have been put at my disposal from which to select cards to illustrate the various chapters. Information on people and events continued to be freely given when I thought I had exhausted all sources. The institutions which made available their collections of Ulster political postcards include the Linen Hall Library, Belfast; the Ulster Museum; the Ulster Folk and Transport Museum; the Armagh Museum; the Museum of the Royal Irish Rifles, Belfast; Just Books, Belfast; and Information on Ireland, London. Individuals who generously lent me their collections include William Nelson, Peter Maloney, Tony Merrick and Fred Heatley; information on some of the current illustrations and publishers was provided by Belinda Loftus; and John Gray kindly let me read his typescript on the 1907 Belfast Strike. Without their courteous aid I would not have been able to lay this work before the reader.

John Killen

9

See page 59 for caption.

See page 95 for caption.

See page 82 for caption.

ONE

THE PICTURE POSTCARD

The picture postcard has become so common that people have largely forgotten its origins of just over a hundred years ago. Like most inventions or innovations it did not spring fully formed from the head of a single genius but evolved from earlier, more formal, attempts to make the benefits of postal communication available to as many people as possible.

The honour of inventing the postcard has been claimed by many people, but social historians agree that the idea of 'postal cards' originated separately and almost simultaneously with two Germans, Heinrich Von Stephan, 1865, and Dr Emanuel Hermann, 1869 (card 1). As a result of their ideas, the first postcard was issued on 1 October 1869 by the Austrian postal authorities. Exactly one year later, on 1 October 1870, the British government, through the Post Office, introduced its own official postcard, a thin buff-coloured piece of cardboard with an imprinted halfpenny stamp, which sold for one halfpenny.

The utility of the postcard was quickly grasped by the business and commercial world which saw in it a much cheaper means of advertising, invoicing and acknowledging payment or receipt of goods than had hitherto been available. The immediate and widespread response to the postcard resulted, among other things, in a prolonged and hard-fought struggle to have the Post Office's postcard monopoly broken. The strength of opinion was such that some concessions had to be made, and from 1872 onwards anyone could print postcards – but with certain restrictions imposed by De la Rue & Co., official printers to the Post Office. These privately printed cards had to resemble in size the official postcards but were to be made of a whiter cardboard and could not bear the royal arms. One side was to be given over completely to the address, and no message was to be written on this side. Initially these cards had to be sent to the Inland Revenue Department to be franked; later, in strict accordance with government regulations, the printer could send batches of cards to this department to be franked before they were delivered to customers.

Almost from its inception the postcard was inadvertently caught up in the political reality of British rule in Ireland. As a result of agreements concerning the delivery of mail between

1. Top right - An example of one of the uses to which early postcards were put. This is a business message from the German publisher, Christian Bernhard, Baron Von Tauchritz, to Messrs. Watkins and Co., booksellers, of St Petersburg, posted on 24 October 1875.

4. Right - Postcards of historic events such as major exhibitions abound. This card was produced and sold at the Franco-British Exhibition, London, in 1908, and was printed as part of a series by Valentine, Dublin. It was posted in 1908.

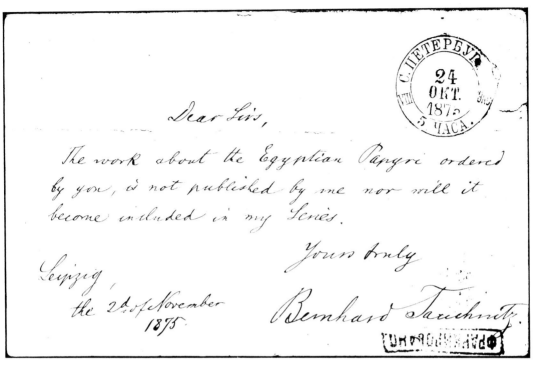

Dear Sirs,

The work about the Egyptian Papyri ordered by you, is not published by me nor will it become included in my Series.

Yours truly

Leipzig,
the 2d of November 1875.

Bernhard Tauchnitz.

Ballymaclinton (Irish Village),
Franco-British Exhibition, London, 1908

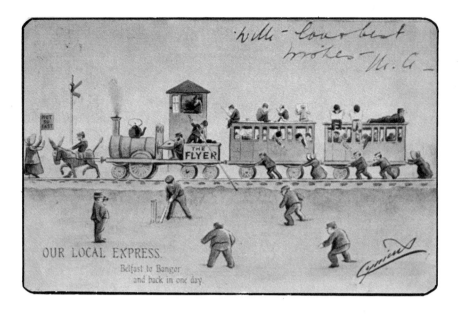

3. Top - This humorous postcard, the work of Cynicus (Martin Anderson), was printed by The Cynicus Publishing Co. Ltd., Tayport, Fife, and posted in 1906. It is one of the 'Our Local Express' series - the basic illustration was capable of being adapted to any area in the British Isles.

2. Above - An early topographical postcard, printed by Lawrence, Dublin, and posted in Belfast in 1906, this card shows the design for the building of St. Ann's Cathedral, Belfast, drawn by the architect Sir Thomas Drew.

At Thiepval, 1st July, 1916.

Charge of the Ulster Division.

" When I saw the Ulstermen emerge through the smoke and form up as on parade, I could hardly believe my eyes. Then I saw them attack, beginning at a slow walk over no-man's land, and then suddenly let loose as they charged over the two front lines of the enemy's trenches, shouting 'No Surrender!'"—*The Times.*

5. This political/patriotic card was published by the headquarters of the Ulster Volunteer Force, Town Hall, Belfast. On the reverse is written:
'And where the fight was fiercest,
And the sternest task was set,
Ulster Struck for England,
And England will not forget.

different countries, Britain printed its first foreign destination card on 1 April 1879. This was a buff-coloured, embossed card, longer than the official inland card, with the words 'Union Postale Universale' printed top-centre. Below this was written 'Great Britain', then '(Grande Bretagne)', and below this again the words 'Post Card'. There was an instant hostile reaction from irate Irish Unionists who informed the post-master general that there was no such political entity as 'Great

Group of Performing Members, Belfast City Amateur Operatic Society, 1913.

6. Published by the Belfast City Amateur Operatic Society and posted in 1913, this theatrical card shows another theme in postcard publishing and is of special interest to the social historian.

Britain'. The mistake was immediately rectified and the caption amended to read 'Great Britain and Ireland'. This long-forgotten episode in postal history acquires a certain seminal importance when one considers the later interaction between the postcard, Ireland and politics outlined in the following chapters.

Not until 1894 did the privilege of affixing an adhesive stamp to one's own postcards devolve to the general public. By that time the postcard had developed from a plain buff-coloured piece of cardboard to a minor art form, for now postcard publishers, especially on the Continent, were beginning to print view cards. The era of the picture postcard had arrived.

The popularity of these view cards was enormous and, with the acknowledged excellence of the German printers by whom many of the early cards were printed, the postcard user became the postcard collector. In Britain by 1895, the Post Office's monopoly was completely broken and independent postcard publishers were able to take full advantage of what was a lucrative and challenging trade. The demand for picture postcards was huge.

7. This humorous postcard is one of a series of Irish Life Studies published by Valentine, Dublin, and distributed widely throughout the United Kingdom. Its romantic portrayal of the Irish character is in marked contrast to later political postcards published by this firm.

As the first decade of the new century progressed, themes in postcard production became apparent. Cards could be arranged into any of a variety of categories: topography, advertising, transport, humour, exhibitions, patriotic, military, novelty, theatrical, political, etc. (2-7). The craze for collecting picture postcards was given added impetus by the increased affluence of a greater number of people who could afford to go on holidays from which they sent back postcards to their relations and friends, not merely to inform them that

'The weather is fine – wish you were here', but to fill gaps in their postcard collections.

THE POLITICAL POSTCARD

One category of postcard much sought after by collectors was, and still is, the political postcard, which commended or attacked politicians, policies, reforms or the lack thereof, providing popular mirth or private embarrassment, depending on one's political stance. Humour and politics are often inextricably bound together in these early political cards, many of which were designed by leading contributors to such magazines as *Punch* and *Vanity Fair*. In this respect, the political postcard is a direct descendant of the political cartoon which was so popular in English society in the first decades of the nineteenth century – the same spirit of social and political satire is evident in both.

In England from about 1900 onwards, publishers of political postcards treated humorously or otherwise themes such as tariff reform, free trade, income tax, the suffragette movement, and successful and unsuccessful politicians – all matters which affected the daily life of their potential customers.

In Ireland, the game of politics has been played at a much more basic level. Since the turn of the present century the fundamental questions of how Ireland is to be governed and how Irish society is to be structured have produced a host of political and social movements whose philosophies and actions continue to influence events in modern Ireland. All have one thing in common: the use of the political postcard as a means of propaganda (8, 9).

In addition, commercial printing and publishing firms quickly saw the economic potential of political postcards and produced many such cards as a fairly safe business speculation. Firms such as Joseph Asher & Co. of London, A. J. Carter of Eastbourne, Carona Publishing Co. of Blackpool, C. W. Faulkner Ltd. of London, and Photocrom Co. Ltd. of London and Tunbridge Wells, published cards denigrating the concept of Home Rule for Ireland in the first twenty years of this century; and contemporary publishers such as the Tolmers Square Co-op of London, Leeds Postcards of Leeds, and Socialists Unlimited of London have used the events of the past fifteen years in Ireland as themes for their cards. As may be expected, however, the greater number of this type of postcard has been printed and published in Ulster's premier city, by

8. This is a fine example of the postcard being used for a political end: a thing now so common that we take it for granted. This postcard, published by Martin and McMurty, Belfast, was part of Thomas H. Sloan's campaign to retain his South Belfast seat in the general election of 1906.

local firms and often commissioned by local institutions. These publishing firms have taken full advantage of the historic events unfolding in their midst, and many of their cards are photographic representations of such things as troops guarding the quays during the 1907 dock strike, the signing of the Solemn League and Covenant 1912, the massive Unionist demonstrations at Balmoral 1914, and anti-H Block marches of 1981. Well-known artists have been employed, or their work adapted, to poke fun and ridicule at the stance of politicians and at political ideologies.

9. The figure of Sir Edward Carson, leader of the anti-Home Rule campaign of the Irish Unionists, graced the postcards of many Irish and British postcard publishers. This postcard was published by C. H. Halliday, Belfast.

Taken chronologically, these cards illustrate the rapidly changing social and political passions and aspirations of a community which has valued its independence highly, but for different sections of which community independence has meant totally different things. Although intertwined and interacting one on the other, the themes and events in Ulster politics will be treated separately here, as they provide natural lines of demarcation.

TWO

JOHN BULL'S FAMOUS CIRCUS
Propaganda of Emerging Sinn Féin

The last years of the nineteenth century and the first decade of
the twentieth saw many rapid changes take place in Ireland.
The Irish Home Rule Party which had been led so ably by
Parnell until his death in 1891 was split in two by the scandal of
their leader's liaison with Katharine O'Shea, the wife of a
member of that party. The depth of ill feeling between former
colleagues, and the viciousness with which it was expressed,
dismayed and revolted a generation of Irish people, resulting in
what appeared to be a general turning away from politics.
Cultural activities seemed to take their place: enthusiasm for
the Gaelic language mushroomed; Gaelic sports were revived
and organised on a national basis; Gaelic traditions and dress
were adopted, and a national consciousness was transmitted
through the drama and literature of a small but highly influential band of poets, artists and writers. These activities, though
non-political in themselves, resulted inevitably in the
heightening of a national awareness which awaited only the
catalyst of powerful personalities to be transformed into political awareness and action. One such personality was Bulmer
Hobson, a Quaker, an Ulsterman and a nationalist.

Hobson was born in Holywood, Co. Down, in 1883 and as
a young man joined the Irish Republican Brotherhood (IRB). In
1902 he formed a boy scout movement which was the fore-
runner of Fianna Éireann; he was active in the Gaelic League,
was jointly responsible for founding the Ulster Literary
Theatre, and became the first secretary of the county Antrim
board of the Gaelic Athletic Association (GAA). In 1905 he and
Denis McCullough, the most prominent of the younger
leaders of the IRB, established the Dungannon Club, of which
Hobson said:

> This club, composed of about fifty young men and boys was
> the most vital political organism I have ever known.
> Without any financial resources save the pence contributed
> by its members, without the influence of a single well-
> known name or any asset save the faith and enthusiasm of its
> members, it set itself the task of uniting Protestant and
> Catholic Irishmen to achieve the independence of Ireland.

**Catching .
Recruits. .**

John Kelly, aged 10, arrested for having "kicked up his feet" and thrown a piece of bread at a woman in the streets of Limerick. He was let out on condition he became a drummer boy in the English Army.

10. This postcard first appeared as a full-page cartoon in *The Republic* on 20 December 1906 and was advertised for sale as a postcard in the same issue. It was drawn by the Belfast artist, Jack Morrow.

The first work of the Dungannon Club was the revival of the anti-enlistment movement. A leaflet entitled 'Irishmen and the English Army' was printed and widely distributed, giving 'some reasons why no true Irishman can join the army of England'. Picture postcards and various other publications were published simultaneously, vilifying recruitment of Irishmen to the British army. The postcard 'Catching Recruits', illustrated by the Belfast artist Jack Morrow, was used extensively to ridicule the activities of the recruiting sergeant, and it appeared subsequently as a full-page cartoon in the second issue of *The Republic* (10, 11).

Throughout his life, Hobson had a penchant for editing and contributing to journals and newspapers, and in 1906 he founded and became editor of *The Republic*, the official organ of the Dungannon Club. This separatist weekly newspaper was printed and published at 114 Royal Avenue, Belfast, and its purpose was threefold: it attacked the practice of British army recruitment in Ireland; it attacked the tradition of nationalist representation at Westminster; and it advocated the adoption of the policies of the emerging Sinn Féin.

the Republic

Vol. I.   December 13th, 1906.   No. 1.

Ulster Literary Theatre.

PRESIDENT—FRANCIS JOSEPH BIGGER, M.R.I.A.

(SESSION 1906-7.)

TWO NEW PLAYS:

The Turn of the Road,

by RUTHERFORD MAYNE.

A Folk-play, the scene of which is laid in a farm kitchen in the county of Down.

The Pagan,

by LEWIS PURCELL.

A Comedy, the scene of which is laid on the slope of the Cave Hill, in the sixth century. . . . .

Ulster Minor Hall,

Monday, Tuesday & Wednesday,

17th 18th and 19th December.

Commencing at 7-45. . . 2/- and 1/-

Constitution of the Dungannon Clubs.

1. That they be open to all Irishmen who endorse their propaganda.
2. That their objects are :—
1. The building up of Ireland
Intellectually—By educating the people by means of Schools, Classes, Lectures, Publications, etc. The establishment of Libraries and every means calculated to educate the country.
Materially—By the fostering of existing and the starting of new industries, by the exclusive use of Irish manufactures and produce, and by nationalised transit services, etc.
Physically—By the popularisation of physical culture and training, by the spread of our national games, and by the training of the boys of the country.
II. The Regaining of the Political Independence of Ireland—
By a passive resistance to the government of this country by any other than the people of Ireland.
3. That they maintain that the attendance of Irishmen at the English Parliament is inimical to the best interests of the Irish nation by admitting the right of any body other than the Parliament of Ireland to make laws binding on this country.
4. That they will co-operate with men of any class or creed who are working for the welfare of the country, *as they believe that the interests of Ireland are above the interests of any creed, or class or party*.

The Office of the DUNGANNON CLUB, is at 114 ROYAL AVENUE, BELFAST.

11. The official organ of the Dungannon Club, this weekly newspaper was founded and edited by Bulmer Hobson and published at 114 Royal Avenue, Belfast. It ran from 13 December 1906 until 16 May 1907.

The National Volunteers in College Green, Dublin, demanding the Independence of the Irish Parliament, 1782.

[*Dungannon Club Series. Printed in Ireland.*]

The Irish House of Commons during the Independence, 1782—1800.

[*Dungannon Club Series. Printed in Ireland.*]

2. This postcard is a copy of a very famous painting depicting the National Volunteers in College Green, Dublin, demanding an independent Irish parliament in Dublin. This demand led to the short-lived Grattan's Parliament 1782-1800).

3. Grattan's Parliament lasted only nine years and was abolished by the Act of Union. This scene, again taken from a famous painting, shows Henry Grattan receiving the cheers of his fellow members of parliament.

'Catching Recruits' was used to illustrate an article entitled 'Surreptitious Enlistment', which read:

The English War Office some short time ago issued an enlistment circular calling for recruits for their cavalry. One paragraph in it reads as follows: 'If applicants so desire it their enlistment will be carried out as surreptitiously as possible.' The dictionary meaning of surreptitiously is, 'without proper authority – underhand or fraudulently.'

The parents of the children of Ireland have now the further consolation of knowing that if their boys – fired and fooled by the blood-and-thunder literature emptied into this country by the ton from England – should think of joining the army of England, the English government is willing to assist them to become its paid slaves 'surreptitiously' – fraudulently and in an underhand manner

The dignity of an Empire that entices deluded boys into its service 'surreptitiously'. No more despicable tactics could be conceived – even by Englishmen.

This postcard is unusual in that it measures five inches by six and a half inches, almost twice as big as an ordinary postcard, and it is the only card of this size published by the Dungannon Club. One can only assume that this innovation in postcard publishing pleased neither the publishers nor the recipients.

Despite the fact that other anti-recruitment articles and cartoons appeared in the pages of *The Republic* throughout its short life, no other Dungannon Club postcard that has survived used this theme.

As Hobson repeated many times in newspaper interviews and in his autobiography, the purpose of the Dungannon Club was to create an intense conviction and a passionate faith, among a necessarily small number of people, that 'the governmental system of England – the armed garrison she keeps in the land – will go down as grass before the reaper before the first generation in Ireland that trusts in itself and starts to work out its own salvation, relying on itself alone.' He believed that the battle was not with England but with the people of Ireland, and that essentially it was a battle for the mind of the nation. The Dungannon Club was involved in a propaganda campaign and as such was the first political organisation in Ulster to adopt extensively the use of the political postcard to help achieve its aims.

The very choice of the name Dungannon Club had a strong element of propaganda in it: the founding members intended to

Dungannon Club Series.

THE BATTLE OF BALLYNAHINCH.

Printed in Ireland.

"And God be praised the pikes were red—before the sun went down,
And God be good to those who fell—that day in Antrim town."
Ethna Carbery.

Dungannon Club Series.   Printed in Ireland.

THE BATTLE OF ANTRIM, 7th JUNE, 1798.

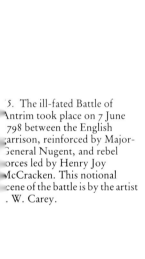

14. The Battle of Ballynahinch took place on 12/13 June 1798 between the King's troops, commanded by Major-General Nugent, and rebel troops commanded by Henry Munroe. The rebels were entirely routed and the town of Ballynahinch sacked and burned by the military.

15. The ill-fated Battle of Antrim took place on 7 June 1798 between the English garrison, reinforced by Major-General Nugent, and rebel forces led by Henry Joy McCracken. This notional scene of the battle is by the artist J. W. Carey.

16. This postcard was designed by Jack Morrow and is a satirical sideswipe at the methods used to gain and to maintain England's colonial empire.

evoke memories of the Volunteer movement of the late eighteenth century and the winning of Irish legislative independence at that time. But Hobson's and McCullough's ultimate aim went much further than this, as is illustrated by the postcards published by the Dungannon Club between 1906 and 1907. These cards extol the winning of an independent Irish parliament by Grattan in 1782 using to good effect the implied threat of force on the part of the National Volunteers (12, 13). This level of independence for Ireland, however, could not satisfy such adherents to the principles of Wolfe Tone as Hobson and McCullough. Tone's statement of his

The STRANGER in the house

The Republican Series.   *Printed in Ireland.*

17. 'The Stranger in the House' was designed by George Morrow, later to make a name for himself in the pages of *Punch.* It depicts a complacent John Bull (England) occupying, without invitation, a comfortable seat in the home of a poor widow (Ireland). The widow and her ragged children watch him in sullen anger from the door.

objects and means influenced the thinking and actions of both throughout their lives:

> To subvert the tyranny of our execrable government, to break the connection with England, the never failing source of all our political evils, and to assert the independence of my country. These were my objects. To abolish the memory of all past dissensions and to substitute the common name of Irishman in place of the denominations Protestant, Catholic and Dissenter – these were my means.

18. 'The Wild Geese', 1907, was designed by Robert Lynd, the artist and essayist, and first published on 11 April 1907. It attacks the Irish Parliamentary Party's pursuit of Devolution for Ireland, and its choice of arena (Westminster) in which to fight.

The Republican Series.   *Printed in Ireland.*

The fact that Tone and the United Irishmen resorted to armed rebellion to break the connection with England did not seem relevant to the situation in Ireland in 1907; still less did it seem relevant nine years later when Hobson, by now Centre of the IRB in Dublin and Quartermaster of the Volunteers, was kidnapped by members of a small group within the IRB on the orders of Patrick Pearse, to prevent him from issuing counter-manding orders which might have called off the Easter Rising of 1916.

The violent means adopted by this small band surprised and

DEVOLUTION PIE.

The Republican Series.   *Printed in Ireland.*

19. Left - 'Devolution Pie' was designed by John P. Campbell, brother of the poet Joseph Campbell. The object of his satire is Devolution, with England (John Bull) depicted as the baker of a (Devolution) pie. The ingredients are PROMISES (from a broken jar), SYMPATHY (also from a broken jar), BRITISH IDEAS (kept in an extremely slender jar), and SUPREMACY (taken from a barrel).

20. Right - 'John Bull's Famous Circus was designed by Robert Lynd and published on 11 April 1907. This postcard depicts the Mother of Parliaments as a circus - with John Bull (England) as ringmaster. Attractions include 'Redmond's sleight of hand', wire pulling by Sir Anthony McDonnell, and 'Birrell's Comic Clowning'. Other humorists, before and since, have used this analogy to represent parliament and politics in general.

shocked Hobson, but their adoption can be seen as a direct consequence of the propaganda of the Dungannon Club a decade earlier, and would have been condoned by the old Fenian chief, John O'Leary, whose image graced one postcard in the set published by Hobson and McCullough (14, 15).

The Dungannon Club constantly attacked England's continued presence in Ireland in a series of articles and cartoons in its newspaper. The Morrow brothers, Jack and George, contributed full-page cartoons, which were later reproduced as postcards, caricaturing the smugness and hypocrisy of England's colonial tradition (16, 17). At the same time the

paper heaped scorn on Westminster, stating in no uncertain terms the folly of looking to English goodwill for a solution to the Irish problem. Postcards were reproduced from drawings by Belfast artists Robert Lynd and John P. Campbell (also contributors to *The Republic*) which poked fun at the modern day 'Wild Geese' who sought concessions from their masters in the English capital (18-20).

Only by vigorous self reliance could Ireland win its independence and if the pages of *The Republic* were anything to go by that self reliance was already at hand. In the issue for 20 December 1906 a correspondent writes:

'The Sinn Féin Movement'
An Englishman has been writing to the English Daily Mail and to Harper's Weekly 'on the Sinn Féin Movement in

Ireland.' He says: 'I bring back from a two months' tour through Ireland no stronger impression than this – that Ireland is becoming Irish. A movement is on foot, broader, grander and more revolutionary than any she has ever known. It is a movement of national resurrection, of national self-realisation and self-dependence. There is no modern miracle more stupendous or more fascinating than the rebirth of an ancient nation. It is nothing less than this that is now being wrought in Ireland. The people are recreating themselves from within. They are recovering their collective soul; they are reviving their racial conscious-ness; they are being swept and invigorated by the returning spirit of essential nationhood . . . Young Ireland, priest and student alike, is rallying to its side, and I conceive the time is not far off when we in England shall be confessing that, compared with Sinn Féin, every other Irish agitation was the merest squib.

The year 1906 saw the Sinn Féin movement emerge from the region of ideals and abstractions into the arena of Irish politics proper with a fully formulated practical policy. It proposed to arrest the anglicisation of Ireland by recovering for the Irish people the management of its education, its agriculture, its industry and its manufacture (21). The Dungannon Club spread this message of national regeneration; the Club's main purpose was to educate the rising generation through its newspaper, leaflets and postcards.

In 1907, Hobson and McCullough reorganised the IRB in the Belfast area and set out to organise Ulster. When the long-standing Ulster representative on the Supreme Council – Neill John O'Boyle of Randalstown – was replaced by the youthful and able McCullough, the scene was set for the revitalisation of what had become an almost moribund organisation. The following year, after the financial failure of *The Republic*, Hobson moved to Dublin to work on W. P. Ryan's weekly newspaper, *The Irish Peasant*.

Although it lasted for only a very limited period of time and reached relatively few people, the Dungannon Club had an effect out of all proportion to its size. The postcards produced by the Club were the work of a small group of Ulster illus-trators whose qualities were later acknowledged in the fields of theatre, book and magazine illustration and landscape paint-ing. The cards are now extremely rare and consequently much sought after by public and private collectors. The insight they

21. 'Sinn Féin and Prosperity', designed by Norman Morrow and published on 11 April 1907, represents the economy of Ireland being ruined and hemmed in by English tariffs. The only hope is to follow the Sinn Féin policy to prosperity.

provide into events of 1912-14 in Ulster and 1916 in Dublin is of great importance. They show that once again northern patriots had given the lead in a national struggle for independence. The message was not lost on the Ulster Unionists who opposed the proposed third Home Rule bill, nor on the southern nationalists who achieved a partial independence for their country by the bloody sacrifice of 1916.

In the immediate future, however, social issues such as wages and conditions of employment seemed more relevant to the populace of Belfast, but sectarian politics, unhappily never far from the surface in Ulster, was the rock on which worker solidarity was to founder.

THREE

MILITARY ON DUTY AT DONEGALL QUAY
The Belfast Strike of 1907

1907 was a year of great social upheaval in the city of Belfast, with the traditional sectarian divisions between workers being breached for a period by the impact of a strike movement led by labour leader, James Larkin. Larkin had been elected General Organiser of the National Union of Dock Labourers (NUDL) in 1906, despite reservations on the part of certain members of the executive of that union. He was so successful, however, at acquiring new members that his appointment, initially on a temporary basis, was quickly made permanent. His first job was to reorganise the union in the Scottish ports, a task which required all his reserves of stamina and resourcefulness. When the Labour Party decided to hold its eighth annual conference in Belfast in January 1907, the union thought that this was a good opportunity to begin the reorganisation of the Irish ports. On 20 January 1907 Larkin arrived in Belfast. Less than a month later he had recruited some four hundred members to the NUDL; by April, the union had over two thousand members in Belfast.

Larkin was a charismatic leader. Self-educated, he used his reading to fortify a vivid imagination. In debate or on a platform his build and flamboyant oratory gave him a hold over his audience which was enhanced by his obvious sincerity. He was driven by a deep compassion for and commitment to the poor – Belfast in 1907 had many such (22). Despite the fact that the industrial magnates of Belfast were enjoying a period of soaring profits and that rates of pay among skilled workers were among the highest in the United Kingdom, unskilled workers faced low wages, poor working conditions and no security in their jobs. These were the people Larkin had come to organise in their fight for a decent living wage. Almost immediately, the discontent among the unskilled workforce became manifest.

On 26 April 1907 unskilled workers at the Sirocco works went on strike for higher wages and members of the NUDL were threatened with dismissal by the Manager of Kelly's Coal Boat Company, and almost the entire workforce walked off the job in protest. Unrest spread rapidly. On 7 May the Belfast Steam-

JIM LARKIN,
Dockers' Organizer.

22. James Larkin was regional organiser for the National Union of Dock Labourers in Belfast in 1907. His portrait was reproduced on many postcards during the dock strike of that year.

ship Company locked out its workers after union men walked off, refusing to work alongside non-union men. The leading Belfast industrialists had been prepared for this, and demonstrated a willingness to fight the trade unions – blackleg labour, organised on an international basis, was introduced. Within two days of the lockout, 150 blacklegs arrived in Belfast from Liverpool, Hull and Glasgow. As they disembarked at Kelly's Coal Quay, striking members of NUDL attacked them, necessitating police intervention which finally restored order (23). Tension rose and tempers flared. Lightning strikes, such as the one at Gallagher's tobacco factory, occurred, and feelings amongst the urban proletariat ran high. On 16 May an angry crowd gathered at Belfast docks, but was dispersed by a force of policemen, four hundred strong. The Lord Mayor, fearing further disturbances, demanded the introduction of troops to the streets of Belfast; two hundred soldiers and four hundred policemen formed a guard at Donegall Quay. Despite the mayor's misgivings no trouble occurred and the troops were withdrawn. Meanwhile all attempts to end industrial grievances by negotiation came to nothing.

By late June 1907 Larkin and the NUDL felt that they had enough support from their followers to issue to the employers a general wage demand of 27s/6d per week for ordinary unskilled labourers and the introduction of a sixty-hour week. Despite earlier success in piecemeal wage negotiation, this general demand was rejected out of hand. As a result, on 26 June 1907, the dock workers struck. Almost immediately three hundred troops were moved on to the quays (24).

The employers lost no time in safeguarding their interests, and next day blackleg labour arrived to man the strike-bound

24. Right -Following the di
turbances of 16 May 190
troops were ordered onto tl
streets to maintain order. Tl
docks area obviously saw tl
greatest concentration
military power and was a frul
ful arena for the postcard phot
graphers. This postcard w
published by J. W. Boyd al
Co., North Street, Belfas

23. This incident in Waring Street was a harbinger of things to come. Tension rose steadily throughout the next few weeks and enterprising postcard publishers were on hand to record them. This postcard was published by J. W. Boyd and Co., North Street, Belfast.

BELFAST STRIKE.—The First Incident : Lamp Uprooted in Waring Street.

BELFAST STRIKE. — Military on Duty at Donegall Quay

25. *Below* - Members of the Royal Irish Constabulary were detailed to escort vanloads of material through the streets of Belfast to their destinations. Within their ranks, however, there was a significant amount of unrest at their role during the strike.

BELFAST STRIKE.—Motor Vans delivering Goods in the Principal Streets of the City under Police Escorts.   Donegall St.

quays. If this situation could not be rectified, the strikers stood to lose everything: not only would their wage demand be lost but their very employment would be terminated ruthlessly by their employers. Help was at hand in the form of a sympathetic strike waged by two hundred Belfast carters who had recently joined the NUDL. Because no-one would remove goods from the docks, work ground to a standstill and goods began to stockpile in sheds and along the quays. By 4 July 1907 all one thousand carters in Belfast were on strike and sixty firms were affected. Police protection and assistance were demanded by these firms and granted to a small number of carts driven mainly by office staff of the firms concerned. As these blackleg carters drove through the streets of Belfast to their various destinations with small police guards, they were often attacked by strikers, their carts overturned and the goods burned (25-28). As preparations for the annual twelfth of July parades gathered momentum, an almost unparalleled aura of calm and worker-solidarity prevailed, in contrast to the usual polarisation of the Belfast working class along sectarian lines. With the good weather and the July holidays in full swing, strike meetings proliferated and were attended by huge crowds of strikers and (often sympathetic) sightseers. The police, forced to attend these meetings to ensure order, were unable to cope with the situation because of their other duties – principally escorting blackleg carters. And, with increasing pressure from the influential band of industrialists most affected by the strike, they had been unable to resist giving an undertaking that a 'large part of the central part of the town is to be protected by the police and military at six points'.

The employers continued to do all in their power to break the strike and on 19 July traction engines were first used to transport goods throughout the city. News of this quickly spread and a large crowd of strikers rioted in Queen's Square. For the next five days the level of violence rose steadily. On 24 July a traction engine carrying cargo from the docks was attacked and destroyed. Widespread rioting in various parts of the city placed an insuperable burden on the police, whose mood was anything but calm. For some considerable time a 'more pay' movement had existed among rank-and-file police whose average weekly wage ranged between 24 shillings and 36 shillings – not much more than that of the bulk of the strikers. Their hours were long and their conditions of service poor, and, as one strike leader told a large gathering, the police would strike for better pay only they dared not. In this analysis he was mistaken, for events were to force certain members of the

27. As the mood of the striker became more sullen, violen incidents increased in number Machinery and merchandis were thrown into the road an often burned. This postcard also published by Walton, i interesting in that the origina photograph was taken by th firm of Baird, Belfast, who wer also postcard publishers

26. The citizens of Belfast too an avid interest in the progre of the strike and often follow the police escorts and strikers a spirit of general curiosit This postcard was published the firm, W. E. Walton, Roy Avenue, Belfast, which al published crowd scenes fro the 1912 anti-Home Ru rallie

BELFAST
STRIKE.

CASES OF
MACHINERY
BURNED NEAR
ALBERT
MEMORIAL.

Walton,
Royal Av.

BELFAST STRIKE. A TRAIN OF MOTOR VANS UNDER POLICE ESCORT.

Walton, Royal Av.

Belfast police force to side with the strikers and to mutiny.

The event which caused the mutiny was the use of police to escort motor vans and wagons on 19 July 1907 (29). On that day, Constable Barrett refused to sit beside a blackleg driver on a motor wagon, and as a result was suspended. Other members of the more pay movement supported Barrett and a petition requesting better pay and conditions and Barrett's reinstatement was forwarded to the police authority for decision within eight days. This challenge could not be ignored, and Dublin Castle reacted swiftly, hurriedly despatching four extra regiments of soldiers to Belfast (30). Significantly none of these was an Irish regiment. On 30 July 1907, 1200 reinforcements arrived in Belfast. The next day the petition of the Belfast policemen's more pay movement was rejected. Barrett was dismissed from the service and six others were suspended. Barrett now openly cast his lot with the general strike movement and on 3 August he spoke to a large gathering on the Custom House steps (Belfast's 'Hyde Park Corner'). After the meeting he was chaired by his supporters, but the mutiny had already failed (31). Many of Barrett's supporters were drafted out of Belfast to remote stations throughout Ireland, to be replaced by more loyal and dependable constables.

While the police mutiny had greatly heartened the striking dockers and carters, they were still no nearer a solution with their employers. A compromise arrived at by a delegation of British trade unionists and representatives of the employers was rejected as a return to pre-strike conditions. As unrest continued, delivery vans from Hughes's bakery on the Falls Road were attacked and burned on 9 August. A confrontation between strikers and police resulted in police injuries and in the introduction of reinforcements – 2,600 soldiers, 80 cavalry and 500 police. Bayonet and cavalry charges were countered by vicious stoning. On 12 August this was repeated and the order to fire on the crowd was given. Two people, Charles McMullan and Margaret Lennon, were killed; neither then nor later was there any doubt that they had been innocent bystanders who had taken no part in the rioting (32). The fact that this rioting occurred on the Catholic and nationalist Falls Road was used by the employers to drive a wedge between the strikers, most of whom were Protestant. This atmosphere of distrust weakened the strike movement, and in the newly begun negotiations terms were agreed piecemeal in an attempt to salvage something from what many viewed as an impasse. By mid-September the strike was over and the employers had won. The agreed terms saw the strikers back at work except for

28. The quality of photograph in this postcard is high and th incident depicted characterist of methods used by the strikers It was published by Walton Royal Avenue, Belfast

those whom the employers refused to re-employ. No wage increase had been granted and security of employment had not been guaranteed.

The events of May to September 1907 provided the theme for many sets of Belfast strike postcards which were printed and published by various local firms, foremost among whom were Walton, Royal Avenue, Belfast, and J. W. Boyd, 44/46 North Street, Belfast. The cards from these sets are good examples of early photographic postcards and give us a very accurate idea of the state of general unrest which prevailed in the city during the strike. One major difference between the 1907 strike cards and the cards produced by the Dungannon Club and later by the anti-Home Rule campaigners is that the former are purely factual representations of historical events – their producers had no propaganda motive but operated on the principle that the postcard-buying public were interested in natural disasters, revolutions and historic events. The photographic quality of the Belfast strike cards varies from set to set, but the amount of useful information to be gleaned from each card is immense. The captions to the cards published by J. W. Boyd, if laid in the proper sequence, provide a good synopsis of the main events, and the cards themselves resemble stills from a silent movie.

BELFAST STRIKE. OVERTURNED LORRY NEAR DOCKS   Walton, Royal Av.

BELFAST STRIKE.—Conveying Goods to the Quay under Police Protection.

The captions read as follows:

1   Belfast Strike –
    The First Incident: Lamp uprooted in Waring Street (23).
2   Belfast Strike –
    Lorry overturned by strikers in Gt. George's St.
3   Belfast Strike –
    Motor waggon and police escort in Donegall Street.
4   Belfast Strike –
    Ex-Constable Barrett Chaired by his Admirers (31).
5   Belfast Strike –
    Military cooks at work in Ormeau Park.
6   Belfast Strike –
    Scene in Queen's Square (35).
7   Belfast Strike –
    Military on Duty at Donegall Quay (24).
8   Belfast Strike –
    Van of paper overturned in Gt. George's Street.
9   Belfast Strike –
    Conveying Goods to the Quay under Police Protection (29).
10 Belfast Strike –
    Maxim gun section of the Middlesex Regiment in Ormeau Park.
11 Belfast Strike –
    Military Guard at Custom House, Donegall Quay.

12 Charles McMullan –
   One of the victims shot in Belfast riots on Monday August 12th 1907.
13 Funeral of Charles McMullan and Margaret Lennon, victims of Belfast riots.
14 Funeral of Victims, Belfast Riots, at Leeson Street (32).

A second, very similar, set of cards in the possession of the Linen Hall Library, Belfast, complements this set published by Boyd. The quality of photography is better, producing more sharpness and clarity of detail but concentrating very much on the same events. No publisher's name or recognisable printer's device is discernible on the cards and the attempt to attribute them to a specific firm has proved fruitless. Two cards in the set are of special interest because of the amount of factual detail they provide (33, 34).

Other cards in this set show the level of military involvement at this time of deepening conflict and tension (35, 36). The army's overt show of strength was greeted with sullen defiance by the strikers, and with an amused curiosity by the young people of Belfast.

A third firm to see the commercial advantage afforded by the strike was Walton, Royal Avenue, Belfast. This firm produced

Left -Large convoys of ~~lor~~ries under police protection ~~be~~came commonplace in the ~~str~~eets of Belfast. This postcard, ~~pu~~blished by J. W. Boyd, ~~N~~orth Street, Belfast, captures ~~th~~e interest shown by the ~~po~~pulace in these historic ~~eve~~nts.

Below - The deployment of ~~tr~~oops and police around the ~~do~~cks was intensified as the ~~str~~ike wore on. This postcard, ~~pu~~blisher unknown, shows the ~~lev~~el of activity in the Frederick ~~Str~~eet area of Belfast.

BELFAST STRIKE.—Frederick Street Guard being relieved

BELFAST STRIKE.—Ex-Constable Barrett Chaired by his Admirers.

*31. Above -*The unease within the ranks of the Royal Irish Constabulary as to their role in the strike found expression in a more-pay movement led by Constable Barrett. In this postcard, published by J. W. Boyd, he is chaired by his supporters after speaking at the Custom House steps.

FUNERAL OF VICTIMS, BELFAST RIOTS, AT LEESON STREET.   J. W. Boyd.

BELFAST STRIKE — Mr J LARKIN, Dockers'
Organizer, Leader of the Strike

33. Above - James Larkin was a familiar figure in the streets of Belfast throughout the summer of 1907 and was an easy target for the cameras of the postcard publishers. No publisher's name appears on this card.

32. Left - The deaths, on 12 August 1907, of Charles McMullan and Margaret Lennon were tragic and unnecessary. Neither had any involvement in the strike movement. Their funeral cortège was followed by a large crowd of mourners and photographed and published by J. W. Boyd.

cards depicting scenes from the strike and from the Unionist demonstrations of 1912 and the anti-Home Rule agitation of 1912-14. The clarity of photographic reproduction surpassed many of the other local publishers and much detail can be seen without the aid of a magnifying glass. On the card entitled 'Belfast Strike. Motor vans delivering under police escort', we can clearly see the wording on the side of the vans, the details

BELFAST STRIKE.—Labour Leaders addressing the Strikers at Queen's Square, Belfast
Messrs M'Keown   Boyd   Larkin   Murray   M'Kessock

34. Above - Open air strike meetings were common during the strike and were sure of good audiences. A photograph of this scene exists in the Ulster Museum but does not have the names of the speakers which are provided on this postcard, publisher unknown.

BELFAST STRIKE.—Scene in Queen's Square.

BELFAST STRIKE.—The "Cigarette" Guard   Cameron Highlanders at Gallaher's Tobacco
Factory

35. Bottom left - As in all such situations where troops are employed to maintain order, the reaction of the populace to their presence differs greatly. Hostility is one reaction, as shown in the faces of some of the crowd in this postcard, publisher unknown.

36. Above -Another reaction is curiosity - the self-conscious curiosity of the young boys and the flirtatious curiosity of the older girls - shown in this postcard, publisher unknown.

of the police uniforms, the cobbled streets and even the wooden spokes of the van wheels (37). A second card in this series, 'Belfast Strike. Overturned lorries, Great George's Street', is of marked social and political interest in that, primarily, it records an incident during the course of the strike, but in doing so captures a representative cross-section of the people affected by the strike, from the strikers themselves, their bare-footed children and distraught wives, to the members of the Royal Irish Constabulary who would soon engage in their own strike movement (38).

In addition to firms, private individuals produced photographic postcards of the Belfast strike. Photography had become much simpler since its beginnings early in the nineteenth century, and the taking of photographs of exactly the same size as postcards was well established by 1907. This was helped by the introduction early in the century of a new camera specifically for this purpose. In March 1904, Hobbies

BELFAST STRIKE. MOTOR VANS DELIVERING UNDER POLICE ESCORT.   Walton, Royal Av

37. Above - The details in this card and the quality of its photography and printing are mute testimony to the importance of postcards to the study of social and political history and events. The publisher was Walton, Royal Avenue, Belfast.

38. Top right - A microcosm of the Belfast strike is contained in this postcard, also published by Walton. All sections most intimately affected by the strike can be seen here.

Ltd., 12 Paternoster Square, London, circulated its photographic catalogue which drew attention to their series of 'Post Card Cameras' by means of which any amateur photographer could produce pictorial postcards (see Appendix C). That people took advantage of this offer is shown by the number of individual cards, obviously real photographs, which are still to be found today. One such card depicts a regiment of soldiers taking it easy in the vicinity of the docks (39).

The Belfast dock strike of 1907 offered a perfect opportunity for trade union organisation on a widespread non-sectarian basis. That this attempt failed showed clearly that, while bread-and-butter issues undoubtedly were of importance, more deeply rooted political issues were the prime movers in the lives of the people of Belfast. Four years later all Ulster was to be engulfed in a campaign which sought to preserve what was seen as the fundamental basis of their lives – Ireland's continued connection with Britain.

BELFAST STRIKE. OVERTURNED LORRIES, GT. GEORGE'S ST.   Walton, Royal Av

39. Below - This postcard, produced by a private individual, was made possible by the introduction of the Postcard Hand Camera into general circulation. On the reverse, in neat handwriting, are the words 'Belfast Strike 1907 - 4th Battalion Middlesex Regiment - stationed at Derry - temporarily at Belfast'.

FOUR

WE WILL NOT HAVE HOME RULE

The Campaign to Maintain the Union

The rejection of Gladstone's Home Rule bill in 1886 was followed by two decades of relative calm in the political life of those Irishmen who supported the union with Britain. Moments of crisis were not lacking during these twenty years, but nothing occurred to cause a re-enactment of the frenzied activity occasioned by the first Home Rule bill.

While the 1893 Home Rule bill and the 1904-5 devolution crisis stirred Irish, and especially Ulster, Unionists to reassert vociferously their uncomprising defiance of any weakening of the union, no one seriously believed that the union could be broken given the strength of feeling which existed on the subject both in Britain and in Ireland. With the passing of the 1911 Parliament Act, restricting the House of Lords' veto on legislation to three sessions, that belief was shattered. Home Rule became once again a major, indeed an imminent, threat. The Home Rule crisis of 1912-14 is brought vividly to life by the contemporary political postcards published by local firms such as Hurst and Co., Fine Art Warehouse, Belfast, and The Ulster Publishing Co., 36 Shankill Road, Belfast, and by British firms such as Corona Publishing Co., Blackpool, and C. W. Faulkner Ltd., London. The fears, aspirations, attitudes and actions of the individuals and groups involved provide the themes to illustrate hundreds of cards.

Opposition to Home Rule was widespread not only among Irish Unionists but also among British adherents of empire. It was feared that legislative independence for Ireland would put in jeopardy the religious freedom of Irish Protestants; that it would cause the immediate collapse of the Northern Irish economy; and (even more important to the British Unionists) it would strike at the very heart of the British empire. These fears were represented on postcards published by W. & G. Baird, Ltd., Belfast; Valentine, Dublin; The Photochrom Co. Ltd., London and Tunbridge Wells; and by Millar and Lang Ltd., Art Publishers, Glasgow and London. The slogan 'United We Stand, Divided We Fall' was very emotive to a nation just recovering from the wounds, both physical and psychological, inflicted by the Boer War (40, 41). On a more

40. *Above* - 'No Home Rule' was the watchword of Irish Unionists and adherents of the empire. In modified and expanded form it was the standard caption on many political postcards of the period. This postcard was published by J. Cleland and Son Ltd., Belfast.

41. *Right* - English postcard publishers saw the commercial (and patriotic) value of the Home Rule issue. This postcard was published by Millar and Lang Ltd., Glasgow and London.

43. *Above* - 'Belfast under Home Rule 1920' is a strangely prophetic postcard given the Government of Ireland Act 1920 which set up the independent state of Northern Ireland. No publisher's name appears on the postcard.

local front 'Portadown/Belfast Under Home Rule' represented, in a fanciful and humorous way, the very real fears of the Irish Protestant Unionist (42, 43).

In 1892 the Duke of Abercorn addressed the Ulster Convention of Unionist Clubs at Balmoral Show Grounds, on the outskirts of Belfast. He coined the phrase 'We Will Not Have Home Rule', asking his audiences to repeat it after him. This rapidly became the watchword of Irish Unionism and, sometimes shortened to read 'We Won't Have Home Rule', was used on a number of postcards published by J. Adams, New King Street, Belfast; H. Courtney, Belfast; John Cleland and Son Ltd., Belfast, and other local firms (44-46). Variations on this theme are numerous among the anti-Home Rule cards which have survived to this day (47, 48).

But how was Home Rule to be resisted and who was to lead the campaign? Ulster Unionists were very fortunate in their choice of leader, although at first glance he seemed a rather incongruous choice: Edward Carson, a Dublin barrister, who overcame many apparent drawbacks to win the hearts of his followers. A southerner who never entirely lost his Dublin brogue, a stern disciplinarian who always seemed to wear a frown in public, he drew loyalty, respect and love from his northern followers by the intensity of his devotion to their cause. His likeness graced the postcards of nearly every contemporary publisher in the United Kingdom, and on every card his facial expression is the same: hair combed back from a high forehead, eyes deep-set and intense, lips set in a scowl and chin jutting out aggressively (49). His chief aide was James Craig, later the first prime minister of the newly founded state of Northern Ireland. Craig was an able organiser of events and people, and stage-managed the impressive Ulster Volunteer Force (UVF) rallies of the next two years (50). In the parliament of Westminster the most active supporter of Ulster's cause was Andrew Bonar Law, an able politician of Ulster extraction who had family connections with Coleraine where his brother practised medicine. A fourth leader was Colonel R. H. Wallace, Grand master of the Orange Order in the county of Belfast (51, 52).

On 23 September 1911 Carson spoke to a large demonstration of loyalists who had gathered at Craigavon, the home town of James Craig. This was the first of many such meetings and rallies, the purpose of which was to unify opposition to Home Rule. Early in 1912 it was decided that the situation required a solemn Covenant between Unionists to stand together in the face of this renewed threat. Craig organised a

42. *Opposite top* - The real fears of Irish Unionists found humorous expression in this postcard published by Valentine of Dublin. Portadown was chosen, no doubt, because of its fiercely Unionist tradition.

44. *Right* - The Duke of Abercorn coined the phrase 'We will not have Home Rule' at the Ulster Convention of Unionist Clubs in 1892. In shortened form it was used on postcards published by J. Adams, New King Street, Belfast.

45. *Far right* - Sir Edward Carson's face graced many postcards. This card, published by J. Adams, typifies Ulster's attitude to the Home Rule crisis.

46. *Above* - John Cleland and Son Ltd., Belfast, H. Courtney, Belfast, and a host of local and English publishers used the caption 'We won't have Home Rule' on their postcards. This card is obviously one of a set published by J. Adams, New King Street, Belfast.

series of meetings to rally support and on 9 April 1912 Bonar Law, Walter Long, Edward Carson and Lord Londonderry addressed a meeting of over 100,000 men in Balmoral Show Grounds. These men represented Unionists from all parts of Ireland, and they marched in columns bearing the name of their district. It was estimated that the procession, sixteen abreast, took three hours to pass the saluting point (53, 54). Other rallies at which Carson was the main speaker occurred throughout the summer of 1912, culminating in his signing of the Covenant in the vestibule of the City Hall in Belfast (55). On that historic day, 28 September 1912, over 470,000 signatures were collected, some even signed in blood. The propaganda impact of this event was immense and postcards showing crowd scenes and scenes inside the City Hall were sent to all parts of the globe (56, 57).

The Ulster leaders, however, recognised that Home Rule could not be beaten by a scrap of paper, no matter how many had signed it. In January 1913 the decision was taken to form a force to be known as the Ulster Volunteer Force, limited to the 100,000 who had signed the Covenant. Sir George Lloyd Reiley Richardson, a retired Indian officer, became Commander-in-Chief, and immediately set about organising the force in the counties. Within a short time a large, disciplined force was drilling regularly, undertaking route marches, manoeuvres and parades. The climax of the UVF parades occurred on 27 September 1913 with the inspection of 12,000 men of the Belfast Division by Carson and Richardson at Balmoral (58-60). But as long as the UVF remained an unarmed force its critics seemed justified in treating it lightly, if not with contempt.

Arming the volunteers was of vital importance, but during 1913 and 1914 attempts to import arms to Ulster had been anything but successful, and money and prestige were lost in the process. The task was entrusted to a man who had for many years been advocating the arming of the Protestant population of Ulster to resist Home Rule. Frederick Hugh Crawford, Director of Ordnance on the UVF headquarters staff, had been a member of Carson's guard on Covenant day and had signed the Covenant in his own blood. He negotiated with the Jewish firm of Bruno Spiro in Berlin for up-to-date, efficient rifles and ammunition, and after much personal hardship and many adventures he succeeded in running 20,000 rifles and three million rounds of ammunition into the ports of Larne, Bangor and Donaghadee (61-65). With the aid of the motorised division of the UVF, the weapons and bullets were safely trans-

47. Fears of economic ruin as a result of Home Rule were very real among the industrialised population of Ulster. This postcard, published by John Cleland and Son Ltd., Great Victoria Street, Belfast, is a plea from the heart of Irish Unionism.

Loyal Ireland

does not require or want Home Rule in any shape.

We implore the people of Great Britain to use their influence to overthrow the forces that would terrorize and ruin the industrious, and drive the country to desolation.

From _____

Printed and Published by John Cleland & Son. Ltd.. 68 & 70 Gt. Victoria St.. Belfast.

48. The fighting spirit and the determination of Irish Unionists not to accept Home Rule is summed up in this somehow poignant postcard published by the Corona Publishing Co., Blackpool.

WHO SAYS WE'RE TO HAVE HOME RULE?

COME TO BELFAST, AND WE'LL SHEW 'EM'

Sir Edward Carson.

PHOTO RUSSELL

49. The typical pose of Sir Edward Carson, leader of Irish Unionism, was reproduced by numerous postcard publishers. This card was published by Valentine, Dublin, from a photograph by Russell.

ULSTER'S LEADER,

LIEUT.-COL. SIR JAMES CRAIG BART., D.L., M.P.

50. Sir James Craig presented a front of stolid, almost dull, dependability to those who were not familiar with his huge organisational ability and his incisive mind. This characteristic pose was published on postcards by J. Johnson, William Street South, Belfast.

51. The leaders of the anti-Home Rule movement were favourite topics for many postcard publishers. On this postcard - 'The Arms and the Men' - published by Valentine, Dublin, we see four of the main proponents of the Union.

52. As in card 51, the leaders of the anti-Home Rule movement - both British and Irish - were popular subjects with the postcard publishers and the postcard collectors. This postcard was published by Valentine, Dublin.

ported to arms dumps throughout Ulster. In this single exercise the UVF had been armed and a major propaganda coup had been achieved. It greatly embarrassed the police and military in Ulster, and despite extensive searching no cache of UVF arms was seized in 1914. The ingenuity needed to ensure the concealment of the rifles gave rise to many jokes and jibes directed against the forces of law and order (66, 67).

One result of the Ulster gun-running was the stimulation it gave to the National Volunteers who would presently organise a similar event near Dublin. By July 1914 Ireland had two opposing organisations, both fully armed. Civil war in Ireland was never nearer than at this time and was only to be averted by the outbreak of the European war in August 1914. Before this event took place the Home Rule bill was to receive its third reading and looked set to be accepted; the only hope that Carson could see was that an amendment to the bill could be added excluding the Protestant counties of Ulster.

In that event Carson was faced with a difficult decision: was the much-talked-of provisional government to be established

53. Below - Public opinion against the proposed Home Rule bill was mobilised by Sir James Craig in a series of rallies throughout Ulster, culminating in the monster demonstration at Balmoral on 9 April 1912. Crowd scenes were photographed and published by Walton, Royal Avenue, Belfast, among others.

The March Past of 100,000 Irish Unionists at the Great Demonstration, Belfast, April 9th, 1912. The Procession, 16 abreast, took nearly three hours to pass the saluting point.

WALTON, ROYAL AVE.

The Great Ulster Unionist Demonstration, April 9th, 1912. Unionist Clubs and Orangemen marching in column, sixteen abreast, past saluting base (the decorated stand in distance); took three hours to file past.
WALTON, ROYAL AVE., BELFAST.

54. Above - The vast con-course came together from all over Ireland, but the majority came from Ulster. This postcard, by Walton, Royal Avenue, Belfast, gives some idea of the regimented organisation of such a number.

in Ulster with the inevitable clash with the military? Through-out May and June 1914 he prevaricated.

During this period he unfortunately incurred the wrath of the Ulster suffragettes (68, 69). In 1913 Carson had promised that, in the event of a provisional government being estab-lished, Ulster women would be admitted to the vote. Reminded of this promise by a suffragette deputation in March 1914, Carson had to go back on his word because other Ulster leaders were not in favour of women's suffrage. This resulted in a wave of mild incendiarism throughout Ulster and personal attacks on Carson. All this was overshadowed by the decision of 10 July 1914, when authority was conferred on the executive of the Ulster Unionist Council to take any action necessary to maintain law and order in the coming crisis – in fact, the long-awaited provisional government had come into being.

Against a rapidly deteriorating European background the king called an all-party conference to try to seek a solution to the Irish question. Asquith, Lloyd George, Lord Landsown, Bonar Law, Carson, Craig, Redmond and Dillon were all present. Debate centred round the proposal to exclude Ulster from the imminent Home Rule Act and broke down when no compromise could be found. By the end of July, war in Ulster seemed inevitable; plans for a *coup d'état* were at an advanced

ULSTER COVENANT DAY, SEPT. 28th, 1912. CITIZENS

56. Above - On 28 September 1912 - Covenant Day - the whole of central Belfast was swamped by Unionists awaiting their turn to sign. This postcard by G. Kennedy, 50 York Street, shows the crowd in front of the City Hall and stretching into Royal Avenue.

57. Right - English postcard publishers also recognised the importance of Covenant Day and produced many cards depicting crowd scenes and scenes inside the City Hall. This card was published by Photochrom Co. Ltd., London.

ING TO SIGN COVENANT AT CITY HALL, BELFAST.

THE CITY HALL. PHOTOCHROM CO LTD COPYRIGHT

Inspection of 12,000 men of the Belfast Division of the Ulster Volunteer Force by at Balmoral, Belfast, 27th .

55. *Below* - The signing of the Covenant remains one of the most emotive events in the Ulster folk-memory. The historic moment when Sir Edward Carson signed his name was captured and published by Hurst and Co., Belfast.

59. *Right* - The discipline shown by the different units of the UVF was remarkable in so newly formed a body. Their march through the city to the general review at Balmoral was photographed by Baird, Belfast, and published by Hurst and Co.

No. 7   ULSTER DAY.   SIR EDWARD CARSON SIGNING THE COVENANT, BELFAST CITY HALL,
28th SEPT., 1912.

ward Carson, and Lieut.-General Sir George Richardson, K.C.B.,
ber, 1913.

58. *Above* - The formation of the Ulster Volunteer Force was an event of vital importance
to the plans of the Irish Unionist leaders. Undertaken by Richardson it was accomplished
in a remarkably short time. Its first general review was attended by photographers such as
A. R. Hogg whose work was later published by Hurst and Co.; Belfast.

U.V.F.—SOUTH BELFAST REGIMENT EN ROUTE FOR BALMORAL, 27TH SEPT., 1913.
Publishers—Hurst & Co., Fine Art Warehouse Belfast.

(6)   The Great Review at Balmoral, 27th September, 1913.   A General View, showing some of the Troops.

Publishers—Hurst & Co., Fine Art Warehouse, Belfast.

60. *Above* - At the Review of the UVF, Sir Edward Carson inspected some 12,000 men on whom he relied for moral (and, if necessary, military) support. This postcard, published by Hurst and Co., Belfast, is one of a set depicting the serried ranks of his troops.

Ulster Gun Running. "Bravo Ulster".
The mystery Ship "Fanny" unloading at Larne Harbour.
Alongside are the Motor Vessel and "Roma" receiving their cargoes
for Bangor and Donaghadee.

GUN RUNNING AT BANGOR, CO. DOWN, APRIL 25TH, 1914.

62. *Above* - Guns and ammunition were landed at Larne, Bangor and Donaghadee and quickly transported to secret depots throughout Ulster. This postcard, publisher unknown, shows a motorised section of the UVF ferrying away the arms.

61. *Left bottom* - On 24 April 1912, the *'Fanny'* stole into Larne harbour with guns and ammunition for the UVF. This successful coup was of vital importance to Carson's plans and was used to illustrate the postcards of many publishers. This postcard was published by Valentine, Dublin.

stage when the outbreak of hostilities in Europe erupted (70, 71).

When war with Germany was declared Carson immediately pledged the Ulster Volunteer Force to fight for England: 'England's difficulty is not Ulster's opportunity' he said to delegates at a meeting of the Ulster Unionist Council in Belfast, and was cheered for his sentiments. The Home Rule Act became law on 18 September 1914 but its implementation was suspended until after the war. By then events in Ireland had made its provisions irrelevant.

The Ulster Volunteers at Drumalis, Larne.   Guiding the Motors along the Avenues.

BRAVO, ULSTER! UNLOADING THE GUNS AT DONAGHADEE.

"After a' the buddies may be richt."

THE ISLANDMAGEE MAN'S CONVERSION TO THE UNIONIST CAUSE.

[An old Islandmagee farmer when given an account of the happenings at Larne on Friday, 24th April, when the gun runners landed 50,000 arms, admitted that "after a' the buddies may be richt" The Islandmagee folk, although Presbyterians, are not very enthusiastic for or against Home Rule.

Yon nicht auld Nancy waukened me and telt me sic a flare
O' licht was ower the Corran, it g'ed her awfu' fricht :
The morn, when telt what happened, A felt it mair and mair
That maybe—aye, just maybe—the buddies may be richt.

A've lived a peacefu' kind o' life, awa' frae war's alarrums
In fechtin' or in quarrelin' A' dinna tak delicht ;
But when A heerd o' what they'd done wi' fifty thousand arms
A' just begun the thinkin' the buddies may be richt.

Aye, the buddies *may* be richt, after a' ye canna tell ;
A'm no Orangeman nor a Tory—mair Liberal a sicht ;
But noo they're organizin' to send Papishes tae ——
Well, all A' say is just a word—the buddies maun be richt.

So, gain' Nancy will alloo it, an' if they'll len' a gun,
A'll gang if iver wanted and be present at the fecht,
An' tak my share o' helpin' to mak the Mickies run,
A'm danged but noo A'm sure o' it—the buddies *maun* be richt.

65. Above - The effect of the gun-running at Larne etc., had a galvanising effect on the Unionist population of Ulster who now had a concrete reason to believe in the viability of their cause.

63. Left top - The efficiency of the UVF gun-running operation showed how disciplined the force had become, and their use of modern methods of transport, as shown in this postcard (publisher unknown) illustrated their practical resolve.

64. Left bottom - The unloading of the guns at Donaghadee was a highly mechanised and efficient affair carried out during the hours of darkness.

SEARCHING FOR ARMS IN IRELAND.

National Events Series]

O'Flannigan climbed upon the back of Murphy, who was down
Examinin' the parts that are contagics to the groun',
And lookin' —" By me sowl," sez he, and said it very neat,
The divil a arm can I b nould but a pair of purty feet."

[No. 21

67. Much sly fun was poked at the members of the Royal Irish Constabulary who failed to find any trace of the illegal arms and ammunition.

In the propaganda war being waged in Ireland between 1912 and 1914 all kinds of printed material were used to put forward the views and aspirations of the different factions. Newspapers, pamphlets, handbills, press releases, postcards and stamps played their part in this battle for the minds of the people. One extremely interesting piece of political ephemera from this period is the adhesive stamp used by Home Rulers to get their message across. These stamps were not legal tender and could not be used to send letters through the post. They were affixed to letters, parcels, packets and postcards in addition to the statutory halfpenny or penny stamp issued by the Post Office (72, 73). These colourful Home Rule stamps were countered by the publication of 'We Will Not Have Home Rule' stamps (74) by the Picture Stamp Co., Scottish Provident Buildings, 2 Wellington Place, Belfast. Thousands of sheets of stamps, ten for a penny, were published, but few have survived.

When armed hostilities finally ceased in Europe on 11 November 1918, the situation in Ireland had changed forever. The Sinn Féin rebellion of 1916 and the bitterness of the War of Independence were to ensure the partial withdrawal of the British from Ireland. The heroic sacrifice of the Ulster Division at the battle of the Somme on 1 July 1916 and the service, gladly given, of the Ulster Volunteer Force to the maintenance of the British empire hardened Northern Unionists' resolve to maintain their connection with England. The Government of Ireland Act, 1920, setting up the state of Northern Ireland, was the culmination of their fight against Home Rule. Thereafter in Northern Ireland the excitement of political manoeuvring ceased, although political hostilities certainly did not cease.

Between the years 1920 and 1968 virtually no political postcards were published, or, if they were published, they were not collected by any individual or institution known to the author. One reason for this dearth of political postcards is that their *raison d'être* had gone. This period in Ulster's history was not one of political innovation; rather it was one of apathy and sterility in the realms of real politics. A battle had been won and lost and the victors saw no necessity to continue that fight through propaganda; the vanquished seemed not to have the heart to continue a struggle which had evidently been lost. Not until the late 1960s did there seem even the glimmer of a hope that political involvement by a newly self-confident Catholic middle class could affect the government of Northern Ireland. With this hope came the need to assert their position by all means possible, and a new era in political postcard publishing was about to dawn.

SEARCHING FOR ARMS IN ULSTER.

AN ULSTER VOLUNTEER: "Sure, don't ye see I've got no
arms, constable?"
CONSTABLE: "They must be hid in the *Ulster*, then."
(About 100,000 rifles and machine guns are hidden in Ulster.)
Historic Events Series]   [*No. 10.*

66. In the aftermath of the gun-running a concerted police search was begun, but to no avail. The humorous side of the whole affair was not missed by the publisher of this card in his Historic Events Series.

69. *Opposite left* - This postcard, publisher unknown, was printed in Saxony and was for British rather than Irish consumption. It looks forward to female suffrage in a Home Rule parliament.

70. *Opposite top* - In the now inevitable event of the passing of the Home Rule bill, Ulster was determined to stand alone if necessary and fight for the Union. The outcome may have been uncertain but their resolve was clearly shown in this postcard by J. Johnson, William Street South, Belfast.

71. *Opposite bottom right* - This powerful image was commissioned and published by Wm. Strain and Sons, Ltd., Belfast, as one of a set of postcards. Its romantic portrayal of Ulster's plight is strengthened by the juxtaposition of the Union Jack and the rifle.

68. The Suffragettes of Ireland felt let down by Carson's broken promise of support for women suffrage. Their reaction to his unpopular stance was hostile and at times violent.

72/73. Top left and right - Of no monetary value, and having no legal status, these Home Rule stamps were a colourful piece of political propaganda.

74. Above - To counter the colourful Home Rule stamps, the Picture Stamp Co., Wellington Place, Belfast, produced its own anti-Home Rule stamps, using the well-known features of Sir Edward Carson to reinforce the message.

FIVE

REVOLUTIONARY GREETINGS FROM IRELAND

Political and Paramilitary Events 1969-1985

Despite the reality of a permanent Unionist majority in the parliament of Northern Ireland and the consequent enjoyment of the fruits of political and social superiority by the Unionist population alone, Northern Ireland on the eve of the present troubles appeared to be about to embark on a period of social, economic and political amelioration. Under the leadership of Terence O'Neill a new-look Unionism was emerging, and his tentative plans for modernising Ulster society were being cautiously welcomed by a growing Catholic middle class eager to participate in Ulster's regeneration. In 1966, following the Malvern Street murder of a young Catholic barman, the reconstituted Ulster Volunteer Force – an illegal Protestant paramilitary force which assumed the title of the Unionist (anti-Home Rule) private army of 1912 – was proscribed. (Augustus [Gusty] Spence, the most famous of the new UVF leaders, was sentenced to life imprisonment for this murder, and passed immediately into Ulster's folklore. This verdict was seen by the Catholic community as an unmistakeable indication of a growing liberalism in Ulster society.) When the Nationalist Party decided to accept the role of official opposition at Stormont, everything seemed to point to the success of O'Neill's stated intention of building bridges between the two communities in Northern Ireland and of obtaining Catholic participation in a constructive government.

These changes, however, were not welcomed by all sections of Ulster society, especially within the Unionist Party where many saw any reforms granted to the minority community as a sell-out. Mounting pressure for reform from minority groups and politicians drew the Ulster premier increasingly into conflict with right-wing members of his own party. When a new political movement came into being in 1967, representing the aspirations of a growing, educated Catholic middle class, a struggle for political power was inevitable. The Northern Ireland Civil Rights Association (NICRA) outlined its aims as: 1 one-man-one-vote in council elections; 2 the abolition of

Dear Friends,

Northern Ireland needs above all a constructive, non-sectarian constitutional alternative to the Unionists. Northern Ireland Labour stands uncompromisingly for citizens' rights and full British standards of living in earnings, jobs, housing and social services.

Only a party which can unite Protestant and Catholic, and has the support of the trade union movement can hope to form a government in opposition to the Unionist Party. The **only** party which has this appeal and this support is the Northern Ireland Labour Party. To support splinter groups, or parties which appeal only to Catholics, is to concede to the Unionists permanent power in Northern Ireland.

Though we pay British taxes we do not enjoy the same standards. We have higher unemployment and lower wages and earnings; we have inadequate housing and no rate relief for lower income groups; we have lower standards of democracy in citizens' rights and electoral law.

I am fighting this election to eradicate these differences: I ask for your support and your votes.

Yours sincerely,   PADDY DEVLIN.

GO FURTHER
VOTE LABOUR
FULL BRITISH STANDARDS
FULL BRITISH RIGHTS
VOTE DEVLIN

75. Above - Paddy Devlin stood as the Northern Ireland Labour candidate in the Falls area of Belfast. He gained the seat with 6,275 votes beating his nearest rival, Harry Diamond (Republican Labour) by 726 votes.

78. Below - Stratton Mills contested the North Belfast Constituency on his record as its sitting member of some eleven years. He was re-elected with a majority of 9,774.

17 Malone Park,
Belfast 9.

DEAR ELECTOR,

This is the fourth election at which I have asked for your support as the official Unionist candidate in North Belfast. This is probably the most important election Northern Ireland has ever faced—do we drift into anarchy or pull ourselves together !

I believe the vital issues in this election are—

1. To demonstrate to the world that despite recent events Ulster is determined to remain an **integral part of the United Kingdom.**

2. That the **security of Northern Ireland** both internal and external should have top priority. On 13th October I warned in the House of Commons of "the continued provocative nature of the enclaves in the Bogside and Falls Road"—the Queen's Writ must run in all areas of the Province.

3. That all sections of the community must play their part in **reducing tensions** and helping to restore normality—a bitter divided Ulster has no future !

4. The **economy of Ulster** has suffered greatly due to recent events. Joint action by the Stormont and Westminster Governments is necessary to restore the momentum of economic development and deal with unemployment.

5. Don't forget that this is a **Westminster election**—do you wish a Conservative and Unionist or a Socialist government to rule the United Kingdom ? Which is best for Britain ? Which is best for Ulster ? I have no doubt that the sooner we can get Harold Wilson out of Downing Street the better for everyone. Socialist policies and attitudes have been harmful to the country and a further period of Labour government would be disastrous !

If re-elected as your M.P. **my special interests** will continue to be—an improvement in the real living standards of old age pensioners, widows and war disabled—an intensification of the housing programme—the Irish Sailors & Soldiers Land Trust —a reduction of high interest rates which hit, especially hard, house purchasers and businessmen —the development of our economy in co-operation with Stormont—the future stability of the Linen industry, Harland & Wolff's and Short Bros. & Harland—a reduction in the crippling burden of taxation and a proper recognition of the role of the small business.

My record. I have been your M.P. for almost 11 years and have endeavoured to actively and forcefully represent the interests of North Belfast and of Ulster in the House of Commons as well as on radio and television. My home and business are in Belfast and I have at all times been readily available to my constituents. Over the years I have helped many thousands of people with a wide variety of problems.

At all times I will do my best to speak and work for the good of Ulster. I ask for your support and your vote on Thursday, 18th June.

Yours sincerely,
STRATTON MILLS.

'gerrymandering'; 3 fair allocation of public housing; 4 repeal of the Special Powers Act; 5 the disbandment of the 'B' Specials. In October 1968 NICRA became international news when a banned march took place in Derry's Duke Street, and several leading opposition members, including Nationalist Party leader Eddie McAteer, were injured in a clash with the Royal Ulster Constabulary. This incident caused a huge international stir and prompted Harold Wilson, then British prime minister, to bring pressure to bear on Terence O'Neill to implement reforms in Northern Ireland. Against growing opposition from members of his own party O'Neill began his reform programme. In the wake of his first batch of reforms he delivered his now-famous 'Ulster at the Crossroads' speech in which he asked for across-the-board support for his reforms and spelt out the dire consequences of their rejection. His plea went unheeded and there were increasing calls for his resignation. In an attempt to consolidate his position he called a general election for 24 February 1969.

When the results came in, O'Neill's reform programme was shown to be under threat. Although the majority of members of parliament who were returned to Stormont supported him, he almost suffered a personal electoral defeat at the hands of the Reverend Ian Paisley, who had campaigned as a Protestant Unionist. The division at the grass roots of Unionism was obvious and O'Neill could now command the support of barely half of the Unionist population. In this election (and in all subsequent elections) the postcard was used as a medium of propaganda by individuals and parties. Election manifestos, slogans, biographical details of candidates, and their photographic likenesses could all be printed inexpensively on cards measuring three inches by five (75).

Two months after his election 'victory', O'Neill was forced to resign in the aftermath of Unionist Party fury over his introduction of one-man-one-vote. He was succeeded as prime minister by his cousin, Major James Chichester-Clark, whose period in office saw a worsening of street violence between the polarised communities, and a decrease in the ability of his government to control overall security in the province. In all areas of Ulster, both urban and rural, graffiti began to appear, reinforcing the ethnocentric political feelings of communities under siege.

Cards 76 and 77, produced by private individuals, illustrate the increasing polarisation of the two communities in Northern Ireland. Card 76 shows the recurring loyalist theme of opposition to the papacy and all that it stands for; it also

76/77. Crudely produced by private individuals, these postcards demonstrate graphically the cultural and sectarian divide which has continued to separate the two communities in Northern Ireland.

indicates a growing willingness to support the rising star of the intransigent leader of the Free Presbyterian Church, the Reverend Ian Paisley. The second card (77) represents the opposing side – it depicts life in the Leeson Street area of Belfast during the premiership of Chichester-Clark. The slogans on the walls indicate the bitterness of feeling among the Catholic population at the alleged one-sided implementation of the rule of law and order.

In June 1970 a Westminster general election was held which had important ramifications for Northern Ireland. The first important development was that for the first time in the history of the state of Northern Ireland, Official Unionists secured only eight of the twelve seats; the second was that James Callaghan was replaced at the Home Office by Reginald Maudling. Candidates in Northern Ireland realised the importance of this election as the messages on the reverse side of their election postcards demonstrate (78).

Just under one year later Major James Chichester-Clark resigned as prime minister of Northern Ireland, disgusted at the ineffectiveness of the British government's security policy in the province. He was succeeded by Brian Faulkner, whose term of office saw the introduction of internment, Bloody Sunday, the alienation of most of the minority community, a marked increase of vicious street fighting and murder, and an investigation into the unsavoury methods of interrogation of detainees. In the rapidly deteriorating situation, British Prime Minister Edward Heath felt he had no option but to assume full and direct responsibility for the administration of Northern Ireland until a political solution to the problems of the province could be worked out in consultation with all concerned. As was to be expected, all shades of Unionist opinion deplored the introduction of direct rule, while most opposition parties welcomed it.

The first secretary of state for Northern Ireland was William Whitelaw (now Lord Whitelaw) who saw his primary task as that of reducing tension in the community. However, faced with the same political and military problems as his Ulster Unionist predecessors, he found little room for manoeuvre. He turned his attention, therefore, to purely political matters: specifically, the political future of the province. In March 1973 the British government published its white paper, 'Northern Ireland Constitutional Proposals'. These proposals recommended that a Northern Ireland Assembly be set up, comprising a legislature of seventy-eight members elected by proportional representation. The electoral boundaries were to be

FOR GOD AND ULSTER   **ELECTION COMMUNICATION**

James W. Gracey

84 Wandsworth Road,

BELFAST 4

**Polling Day, Thurs., 28th June,
8 a.m. — 8.30 p.m.**
Your election number is on your official
Poll Card and also where you vote.

79. *Above* - The Democratic Unionist Loyalist Coalition gained eight seats in the 1973 Assembly Election. Mrs. Eileen Paisley was elected to represent East Belfast with a poll of 5,518.

80. *Below* - In South Down, Brian Faulkner, leader of the Official Unionist Party, topped the poll with 16,287 first preference votes. His election literature was printed by the 'Down Recorder' and published by John McRobert, Downpatrick.

**N.I. ASSEMBLY ELECTIONS
CONSTITUENCY OF SOUTH DOWN**

Polling Day: **Thursday, June 28, 1973**

Time: **8.00 a.m. to 8.30 p.m.**

**Vote for FAULKNER and the other
OFFICIAL UNIONIST Candidates**

ELECTION COMMUNICATION

————————

————————

————————

81. *Opposite top* - Recently released from prison on health grounds, Gusty Spence at the time of publication of this card was the best-known leader of the revived UVF.

82. *Opposite bottom* - Photographed and published by Christine Spengler, this card shows a soldier taking what cover he can in the doorway of a terrace house in an unspecified area of Belfast.

83. *Above* - Spengler's photographs of children playing in the midst of riots and security operations highlight the dichotomy of normality in abnormal circumstances.

those of the twelve Westminster constituencies and the election was to be held on 28 June 1973. Because of deep divisions within the loyalist population, party labels were often very poor indicators of the attitude of the candidate towards the white paper which essentially envisaged a partnership government. A confusing conglomeration of parties contested the election, including Official Unionists, Unionist Anti-White Paper Candidates, Democratic Unionists (DUP), Coalitionists, Independents, Republican Labour, Dedicated Loyalists and others (79, 80).

When the results came in, the Unionist Party, for the first time in a Northern Ireland general election, did not command a majority of seats. Also for the first time, no Nationalist Party candidate was elected; the Social Democratic and Labour Party (SDLP), with nineteen seats, established itself firmly as the main opposition party. Around this time a postcard was published (possibly by the UVF) to help reaffirm the staunch loyalist tradition of simple majority rule in Northern Ireland. It shows the UVF leader, Gusty Spence, in uniform in the Maze Prison, holding the flags of the UVF and the YCV (Young Citizen Volunteers). Distributed widely at the time, it is now quite rare (81).

On 18 July 1973 the Northern Ireland Constitution Act became law. It allowed for the devolution of legislative and executive powers if the secretary of state considered this to be in the best interests of stable government. The Northern Ireland Executive was to consist of the chief executive, heads of department and any other persons appointed by the secretary of state: the overall size being limited to twelve. In October William Whitelaw began preliminary talks with the Unionist, SDLP and Alliance parties on the setting up of this power-sharing Executive. In December he was replaced by Francis Pym in a Cabinet reshuffle, and in the same month members of the British and Irish governments met at Sunningdale to discuss, *inter alia*, a Council of Ireland. Immediately, right-wing Unionists protested against this 'blatant betrayal of their birthright'. The Executive, duly constituted, was to last only five months, never recovering from the Westminster general election of 28 February 1974 which had been called by the Conservative government because of the miners' strike.

Right-wing loyalists and anti-Sunningdale Unionists banded together to fight the election as the United Ulster Unionist Council (UUUC), giving approval to one candidate in each constituency to fight the election on the principle of total opposition to the Sunningdale Agreement. As the results were counted, only Gerry Fitt (SDLP) on the pro-Sunningdale side

84. Eleven years on, the boy in the foreground would be about seventeen and the girl about twenty-three. How have the events of the last eleven years affected them and their attitudes to life?

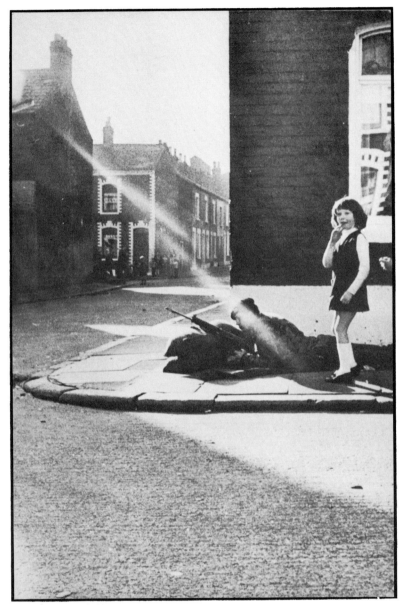

86. *Above* - A child walks past a soldier lying on the pavement behind the meagre protection of three sandbags. Spengler's strength lies in her ability to shock by showing reality.

85. *Opposite* - Random searching was carried on extensively in Republican areas of Belfast and Derry. Many did not accept it as happily as these schoolchildren.

was returned. The UUUC won the remaining eleven seats, a clear vote of no confidence in the new administration.

In May 1974 the newly formed Ulster Workers' Council (UWC) organised and co-ordinated a province-wide strike which led to the collapse of the power-sharing administration. The UWC's main demand was for the dissolution of the Assembly because it was felt that a newly elected body would proclaim the widespread opposition to the Sunningdale Agreement which the recent election result had made clear. Faced with such widespread opposition, on 28 May 1974 the Executive collapsed; a day later the Assembly followed suit. It was clear that there was little possibility of reconstituting the Assembly at any date in the future; consequently, a government white paper was published in July which proposed the election of a Constitutional Convention to consider the best way to govern the province. Since time was required to formulate party policy on any future form of government, it was decided to delay any election to the Convention for some months.

In September 1974 a set of postcards depicting everyday life in Belfast and Derry appeared for sale. There were originally twelve cards in the set, photographic reproductions of street scenes at a time of high political and social tension (82-87). They show scenes of rioting and of army activity in some of

Ulster's most strife-torn streets, and were the work of the French freelance photographer Christine Spengler, who spent four years working in the province. At the time of their publication there was a general outcry against them. Businessmen and clergymen in Belfast spearheaded a public campaign to have the cards removed from shops in the city centre. The Northern Ireland Tourist Board and the City Traders' Association banded together to attack them, and a leading churchman claimed their publication was a 'disgraceful and insidious act which will warp the minds of our next two generations'. Such is the power of the postcard!

Today those cards seem somehow dated, although the same pictures can still be taken in the streets of Ulster's two main cities. Looking at them now provokes a feeling of sadness, possibly because of the constant reminder of the effect that the 'troubles' have had on a generation of Ulster's children.

When the elections to the Constitutional Convention were held on 1 May 1975 they were conducted by proportional representation for seventy-eight seats based on the twelve Westminster constituencies. The UUUC, embracing Official Unionists, Democratic Unionists etc., were firmly committed to 'British standards' of government as can be seen from the election postcards; parties which had been involved in the power-sharing Executive, such as the Northern Ireland Labour Party, stressed partnership government in their election postcards (88).

In a poor turn-out to the election, UUUC candidates polled 55 percent of the first-preference votes, the other seats going to the SDLP, Alliance, the Unionist Party of Northern Ireland and the Northern Ireland Labour Party. As was to be expected, the deliberations of the Constitutional Convention came to nought. The political aspirations of the parties involved were too divergent for any effective compromise to have been worked out. In March 1976 the Convention ceased to exist and no major new political initiative was contemplated. The then Labour government undertook a holding operation in Northern Ireland.

In September 1976 Roy Mason became secretary of state for Northern Ireland. His appointment was rather unexpected and was regarded by many as indicating a tougher British attitude towards the implementation of direct rule. Mason attempted to introduce voluntary censorship of news in certain areas, notably in cases which concerned allegations of ill-treatment directed against the Royal Ulster Constabulary (RUC). During 1977 the security forces increased the level of their activity and

87. For the soldier, a dead serious and highly dangeous routine patrol; for t children, the chance to photographed - for wh purpose they knew ne

Polling Day : Thursday, 1st May *1975*
7.00 a.m. till 10.00 p.m.

VOTE

| **1** | **BRADFORD** |

OFFICIAL ULSTER UNIONIST
Your Number is *5642/43*.

H. & Q.E. Strain,
18 Castlehill Road,
Belfast 4.

88. The Unionist parties in this election stressed their commitment to British parliamentary standards and their rejection of power sharing. Roy Bradford, Official Unionist candidate in East Belfast, failed to reach the quota.

89. *Above* - 'Sensory Deprivation, Palace Barracks, Belfast' was published by Peter Kennard in a set of six photographs using the technique of photo-montage.

90. *Opposite top* - In a turnout of 57% of the electorate, John Hume got 24.6% of the total votes cast. A supporter of the ideals of the EEC, he continues to represent Northern Ireland in Strasbourg.

many arrests were made as the result of information received from suspects and prisoners. Earlier methods of acquiring information was the theme of a postcard published by London-born Peter Kennard. In January 1978 the European Court of Human Rights ruled that five techniques of interrogation employed by the security forces in Ulster constituted inhuman and degrading treatment and that this had been carried out at Palace Barracks, Holywood, Co. Down, at Ballykinlar and at Girdwood Park Barracks. As a result of this finding an undertaking was given that 'interrogation in depth' (including the technique of sensory deprivation) would never

THE CANDIDATE

WHO IS QUALIFIED FOR THE JOB

* A steady, proven and respected record of public service.

* The candidate most experienced in European and International affairs, with an existing international reputation.

* Special adviser for past two years to E.E.C. Commissioner, a post that involved wide contacts and experience of the workings of the E.E.C.

* A fluent French speaker — an essential to do an effective job.

* Former Minister of Commerce.

* Member of the largest and most influential grouping in the European Parliament — the Social Democrats.

"John Hume is one of the most creative political leaders of our generation, a man of outstanding wisdom, courage and understanding."

— Senator Edward Kennedy, New York, May 1976.

THE E.E.C. NOW INFLUENCES OUR EVERYDAY LIVES. WE NEED A RELIABLE VOICE THERE.

JOHN HUME S.D.L.P.

91. *Below* - RVH workers support the men in the H-Block. This banner was carried in many marches in Belfast and Derry protesting against conditions in the H-Blocks of the Maze prison.

again be used in Northern Ireland. Taking this as a theme, Kennard published a card entitled 'Sensory Deprivation, Palace Barracks, Belfast' as one of a set of six depicting apartheid in South Africa, mining conditions in Yorkshire, the Junta in Chile, dioxan poisoning in Seveso, and psychiatric repression in Moscow. His cards attempt to produce a visual shock by means of photomontage – joining images together into one picture. The postcards are larger than normal so that they can be displayed as complete images and not as mementos (89). This rather chilling image (or juxtaposition of images) evokes something of the disorientation of the subject under sensory deprivation.

Mason's period in office saw the struggle by republican and loyalist prisoners for 'special category' status which had been withdrawn in March 1976. This led to the 'blanket protests', where prisoners refused to wear prison garb in furtherance of their demands. It also saw the handing over of routine patrolling to the RUC, and a general tightening up of security. Economic innovations (such as the setting up of the ill-fated De Lorean project) were eagerly sought in an attempt to make direct rule more acceptable socially and economically. However, violence continued. The verdict of the European Court of Human Rights showed that torture had been condoned by those in authority; and the prison protests continued. The Labour government, already tottering, faced a vote of no confidence in March 1979 and lost by one vote, Gerry Fitt abstaining. The next day a general election was announced. It was held on 3 May 1979 and all parties in Northern Ireland competed.

Traditional voting trends were adhered to. In round figures the total Unionist vote represented about 60 percent of the total votes cast, and the nationalist vote about 30 percent. Official Unionists won the majority of seats; the Unionist Party of Northern Ireland fared disastrously, winning only 1 percent of the total vote and no seats, while, once again, fringe parties such as the Northern Ireland Labour Party were virtually ignored by the electorate.

Within a month of the general election the voters of Northern Ireland were at the polls again. The election to the European Parliament, held on 7 June 1979, was of great importance to a small, mainly agricultural community such as Northern Ireland. It was also seen by the Official Unionists as a chance to show the true allegiance of the loyalist community, the majority of whom had supported Official Unionist candidates in preference to Democratic Unionists in May. The

92. An aerial view of H-Blocks of the Maze pri with superimposed pho graphs of Republi prisoners 'on the blank

93. Riot shields, helmets, gas and rubber bullets w used as means of crowd con and dispersal during the vola period of the hunger str

The British way of life in Ireland

Bobby Sands

94. *Above* - Bobby Sands, commanding officer of the Republican prisoners in the Maze prison, went on hunger strike on 1 March 1981 and died on 5 May 1981 after sixty-six days, aged 27.

95. *Opposite top* - During the hunger strike, riots and civil disorder worsened and Republican sympathisers attacked the security forces with renewed ferocity.

96. *Left* - May 1981 saw the tragic deaths of two young girls who had been struck and fatally wounded by soldiers firing plastic bullets. The campaign to have these weapons banned continues today.

European election was seen as a direct choice between the Official Unionists and the Reverend Ian Paisley. There is no disputing the fact that the loyalist community voted for Paisley. All shades of political opinion contested the election which resulted in the three Northern Ireland seats being filled by the Reverend Ian Paisley (DUP), John Hume (SDLP), and John Taylor (Official Unionists) (90).

The remainder of 1979 and 1980 saw the security situation and the economy of Northern Ireland go from bad to worse. The conditions of the republican prisoners in the H blocks of the Maze Prison were causing increased concern among the nationalist community, and agitation and protests escalated throughout the province (91, 92). In November 1980 seven 'blanket men' in the Maze Prison went on hunger strike to achieve their demands:

1   the right to wear their own clothes
2   the right to refrain from penal work
3   the right to free association
4   the right to organise their own educational and recreational facilities, and to one letter, visit and parcel per week
5   the right to full remission of sentences.

As the hunger strike continued through December the protest marches grew in size, often approaching the numbers of the civil rights marches of a decade earlier. Concessions were not forthcoming but a compromise solution seemed to have been achieved between the hunger strikers and the authorities, with the prisoners apparently being allowed to wear their own clothes and not prison uniforms. This soon proved to be a misconception, and a second hunger strike was called by the commanding officer of the republican prisoners, Bobby Sands. Amid growing community fear, and as the hunger strikers were allowed to die, rioting in Belfast and Derry got steadily worse (93-95). The almost tangible tension surfaced within the minority community with the deaths of two young girls who had been struck and fatally wounded by plastic bullets fired by troops trying to contain the rioting (96). On the day that Carol-Ann Kelly was fatally wounded, five members of the Royal Green jackets were blown up and killed near Camlough, Co. Armagh. The Provisional IRA stepped up their campaign of bombings, shootings and patrolling, and intensified their propaganda campaign (97-100).

Protest against the British government's intransigent attitude to the hunger strikers was voiced in England as well as

97 to 100. Opposite and page 9. The Provisional IRA took series of photographs of the men in patrol and comb situations in a propagan exercise to show that th could move freely with Northern Irelan

Revolutionary
greetings
from Ireland

Revolutionary
greetings
from Ireland

Revolutionary greetings from Ireland

Revolutionary greetings from Ireland

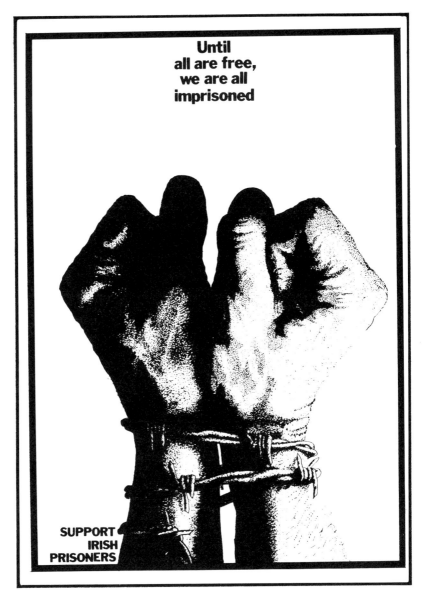

101. This postcard was published by Socialists Unlimited, London, using graphics provided by 'Information on Ireland'.

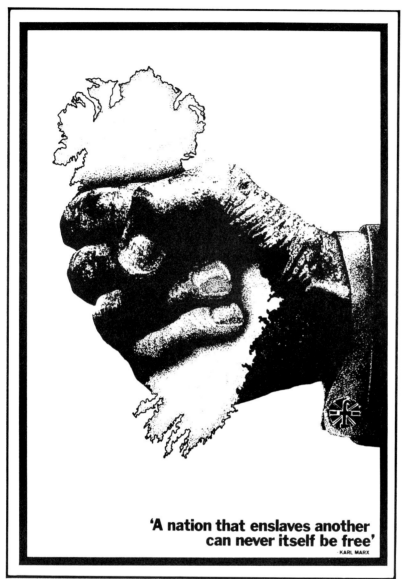

'A nation that enslaves another
can never itself be free'
·KARL MARX

102. As with the previous card, this was published by Socialists Unlimited, using graphics provided by 'Information on Ireland'. It quotes Marx to reinforce the message.

in Ireland. Information on Ireland, an organisation based in London which advocates British withdrawal from Ireland, published an indictment of British prison policy in the North of Ireland entitled *The H Blocks*, and illustrations used in the pamphlet were reproduced as postcards castigating Britain's continuing involvement in Ireland (101-103).

Media coverage of the troubles was also attacked. The complacency of the majority of British people to the tragedy of Northern Ireland, and the alleged cause of that complacency (media censorship), were used at this time as themes for two

Britannia waives the rules

103. This postcard, published by Socialists Unlimited from graphics again provided by 'Information on Ireland', paraphrases the words of 'Rule Britannia' to sum up the reality of English rule in Northern Ireland.

cards published by British firms (104, 105). The design on card 105 was first used in a pamphlet entitled *The British Media and Ireland*, published by Information on Ireland, and reprinted as a postcard. The pamphlet alleges that over thirty television programmes about Ireland have been banned, censored or delayed over the past ten years, that books and magazines have been withdrawn and pulped, that the content of newspaper articles on Ireland is constantly vetted and that the pressure on journalists to conform is intense.

Given this increased level of anti-British propaganda, the

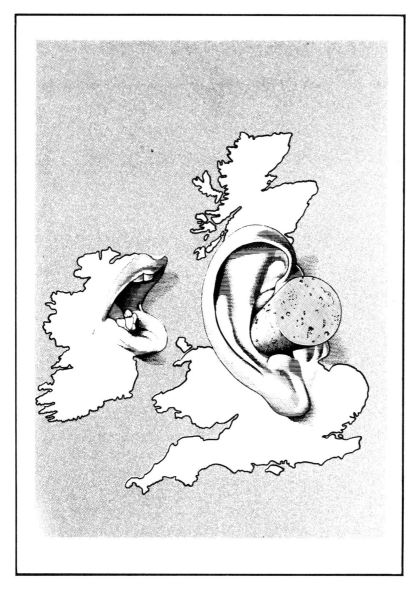

104. Left - The complacency of most people in 'mainland Britain' when confronted with the tragedy of Northern Ireland is ridiculed in this card published by Leeds Postcards.

105. Right - The continuing accusation of media censorship is scathingly illustrated in this postcard published by Leeds Postcards. Graphics from 'Information on Ireland' and produced by Socialists Unlimited.

republican movement was eager to use the major political crisis over the Falkland Islands as a stick with which to beat Britain; the parallels between the situation in the South Atlantic and in Northern Ireland were too obvious not to have been exploited (106).

In July 1983 Just Books, a radical Belfast bookshop/ cooperative, published a set of postcards very reminiscent of those produced by Spengler almost a decade earlier. They represent the camera work of many local and visiting journalists and are mute testimony to the inevitable hardening of attitudes which had taken place in the intervening years

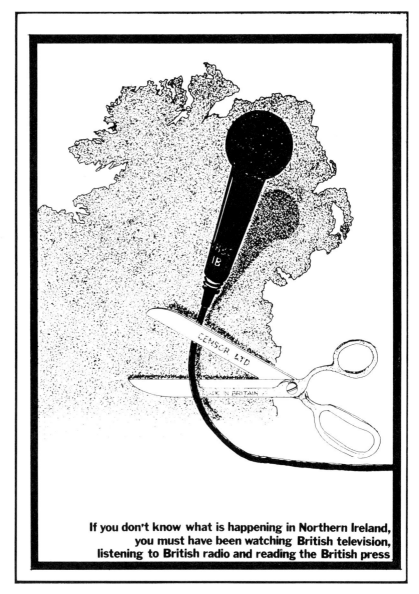

If you don't know what is happening in Northern Ireland, you must have been watching British television, listening to British radio and reading the British press

(107-109).

A recurring theme depicted in this set of cards (reprinted in July 1984) is the use of plastic bullets by the security forces. The debate as to whether their use in Northern Ireland should continue raged throughout 1984, with the picketing of the Brocks factory in Dumfrieshire where they have been made since the American ban on their export (110-111). Also attacked in this set of postcards is the practice of strip searches of inmates and visitors to Northern Ireland's jails, particularly Armagh's Women's Jail (112). This practice, to stop the smuggling in of weapons or drugs to inmates, has been

108. Above - This photographic postcard shows a youth using a catapult to fire metal objects at the security forces. Published by Just Books, it is obviously the inspiration for the wall mural depicted in the previous postcard.

107. Left - This postcard shows a wall mural in Moira Street, Belfast, and quotes the words of Bobby Sands who died on hunger strike in 1981.

106. Opposite top - Cormac, the popular radical cartoonist, uses the Falkland crisis to justify the raison d'être of the Provisional IRA in Northern Ireland.

A PLASTIC BULLET IS A SOLID CYLINDER OF PVC

IT SMASHES HEADS

110. Above - The continued use of plastic bullets in Northern Ireland has been attacked by many individuals and groups. This postcard, published by Leeds Postcards, Leeds, makes the basic statement 'A plastic bullet is a solid cylinder of PVC'.

109. Opposite top - A soldier points his weapon at a group of teenagers crossing a common. It is hard to say whether he is posing for the camera or whether he is in danger.

112. Left - Strip searching of visitors to Ulster's jails has been a major bone of contention between prisoners' families and the authorities for years. Women's groups have been particularly active in condemning the practice.

111. Plastic bullets (or batton rounds) are standard instruments of riot control in Northern Ireland. This postcard, published by Just Books, shows two soldiers taking aim.

attacked by women's groups, republican spokesmen and members of the Roman Catholic hierarchy in Ireland. As recently as November 1984 Bishop Cathal Daly, Bishop of Down and Connor, attacked strip searches in a sermon in the Pro-Cathedral in Dublin, describing the practice as 'degrading to its victims and distasteful to those who conduct it'.

The present 'troubles' in Northern Ireland show no sign of solution. No doubt subsequent events will produce further political postcards, which in turn will be used to illustrate the history of a lost generation.

SIX

WIT AS A WEAPON
Ulster Politics 1905-1985

> By making our enemy small, inferior, despicable or comic
> we achieve in a round about way the enjoyment of over-
> coming him. . . A joke will allow us to exploit something
> ridiculous in our enemy, which we could not, because of
> obstacles in our way, bring forward openly. . . Tendentious
> jokes are especially favoured in order to make aggressiveness
> or criticism possible against persons in exalted positions
> who claim to exercise authority. The joke then represents a
> rebellion against that authority.
>
> *Jokes and the Relation to the Unconscious,* Sigmund Freud

Jokes and jibes at authority may not topple administrations or
bring into existence a new social order, but they have certain
functions within any political framework. The victims of the
political joke have no defence against it – if they retaliate they
succeed only in making themselves look more ridiculous. The
shortcomings of a government or the fallacies of an enemy can
often be best highlighted by means of a joke or caricature,
which at the same time can be used to reinforce one's own
position.

The (no doubt unconscious) application of this theory of
Freud gave rise to a genre within a genre in postcard publishing. Native Irish wit and satire combined to produce many
humorous political postcards dealing with the aspirations and
events during the period 1905 to 1985. Most of the major
publishers of Ulster's political postcards produced this type of
card. The Dungannon Club made good use of artists John P.
Campbell, Jack Morrow and George Morrow to design cards
ridiculing devolution, English imperialism and the Irish
Parliamentary Party; while Johnson, the Belfast publisher,
used local artist George Lemon to ridicule Home Rule, and
Joseph Asher and Co. of London used designs by the famous
postcard illustrator Donald McGill to ridicule the Irish situation in general (113-115).

Verse (of a sort) was used to poke fun at the leading politicians of the day (116). This postcard, 'The Budget and Home
Rule – or – Mr. John Redmond's appeal to Mr. Wm. O'Brien',
attacks Redmond's support for the budget proposals of 1909

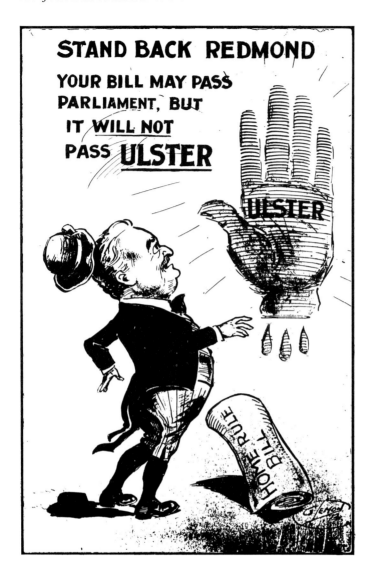

which were rejected by the House of Lords; this rejection
opened the way for a determined onslaught on the privilege of
the Lords by the then chancellor, Lloyd George. His attack led
to the 1911 Parliament Act which restricted the veto power of
the Lords to three sessions and in effect opened the way for
Home Rule, a measure greatly feared by the Ulster Unionists.

It was firmly held in Ulster, and farther afield, that Home
Rule for Ireland would mean the subjugation of Protestantism
by Roman Catholicism, the death of the Ulster economy and
the break up of the empire. The cards 'Portadown and Belfast
under Home Rule' (see cards 42, 43) illustrate the conjectured
effects of Irish independence on the industrial north, while the

The Budget and Home Rule

OR

Mr. John Redmond's Appeal to Mr. Wm. O'Brien

————— ◆ ▶ ◆ ◀ ◆ —————

Och Mister O'Brien, ye needn't be tryin'
  To make people think I'm a fool ;
If I vote for the Budget, there's no one will grudge it,
  Provided it leads to Home Rule.

Mind, we've got a quare task, with the help of Friend Asquith
  (I say " Friend," but really mean " tool"),
The Lords must be mended, suspended, or ended,
  Or ne'er will we get our Home Rule.

That poisonous Veto, like sting of mosquito,
  Must go, though it takes a hard pull.
We'll have to be cautious, though the Budget is nauseous—
  Gulp it down, or we'll not get Home Rule.

And we must work together, so stop all this blether
  About " Independence," my Jew'l.
If you and I quarrel, it's not in this worl'
  We ever will get our Home Rule.

So, William O'Brien, let's have no more shyin',
  Together let's go for their wool.
If you back my endeavour, I'll thank you for ever,
  And reward you—when we get Home Rule.

So keep up your pecker, the Irish Exchequer
  Will give you the Chancellor's stool,
You can play " ducks and drakes" with all Ulster makes
  To amuse you when we get Home Rule

Then never mind hardships—let's murder "Their Lardships"
  And defy the ould tyrant, John Bull.
They'd better take care of us—here comes the pair of us.
  Hooroush ! clear the way for Home Rule.

With a thumpin' shillalah, we'll go for them gaily,
  And whack their numskulls somethin' crool.
Then we'll tread on the tails of both England and Wales,
  And see how they like our Home Rule.

Nicholson. Printer. 76 Church Lane

116. Above - The safeguard of the Union was the power of the House of Lords to veto any legislation from the Commons at will. With the passing of the 1911 Parliament Act this veto was nullified. The situation is humorously expressed in this card, published by Nicholson, Belfast.

113. Left - George Lemon provided illustrations for local magazines and some of his work was published in postcard form by the firm of Johnson, Belfast. John Redmond, Home Rule, Ulster and Westminster are all treated in this card.

Men, keep your Rifles free from Rust!

Let Ulstermen determined stand
Against Home Rule with heart and hand,
Or Rome her rule will on us thrust ;—
Men, keep your Rifles free from rust !

Rouse, Ulstermen, in vale and hill,
Be up and active—Drill, drill, drill !
Our Leaders tell us that we must ;—
Men, keep your Rifles free from rust !

That dear old Flag, the Union Jack,
Fight for its honour back to back ;
Dare Rebel tramp it in the dust ;—
Men, keep your Rifles free from rust !

The Jesuits, through Redmond's mouth,
Speak to their dupes in West and South :
"There's gold up North, no more dry crust";
Men, keep your Rifles free from rust !

We know what Rome did in the past,
When Spain her great Armada massed :
It came to glut her bloody lust ;—
Men, keep your Rifles free from rust !

King William at the glorious Boyne,
Our Fathers did his forces join,
And through King James's army burst ;—
Men, keep your Rifles free from rust !

The Freedom that our Fathers won
On bloody field midst crash of gun :
God did them help, their cause was just;—
Men, keep your Rifles free from rust !

(COPYRIGHT).   J.P.G., Belfast.

The Exchange Publishing Co., 36 Shankill Road, Belfast.

117. Above - 'Home Rule is Rome Rule' has been the watchword of Unionist leaders for many decades. It is used here to exhort Ulstermen to drill and train in preparation for the fight to preserve their freedom.

120. Right - The bulldog and the cur - illustrated in card 119 - is the theme of this anti-Home Rule postcard published by the Ulster Publishing Co., Belfast.

121. *Above* - Once again, the 'bulldog and the cur' theme is used in this postcard published by the Ulster Publishing Co. Its illustrator - W. Watson - illustrated other fine cards for Ulster publishers.

Sir Edward Carson's Bulldog "Ulster."

A Bulldog met a cur,
    Who tried to steal his bone ;
The Bulldog said, please go away,
    Leave me and mine alone.
The Cur said, I'm a Roman dog,
    Forbye John Redmond's pet ;
If that be so, the Bull replied,
    You're not much good I bet.

Now I'm Sir Edward's bulldog,
    And Ulster is my name ;
So if you don't be off, sir,
    I'll not warn you again.
You want to steal my property,
    This bone I've fairly got ;
While I work might and main, sir,
    You belong to a lazy lot.

Don't tempt me to fight,
    Or my industry to kill ;
Or you'll swallow your Ne Temere.
    Likewise your Home Rule Bill.
I'll inspect your Convents,
    If you touch my Bon-r Law ;
And I'll smash up your confession box
    With one blow of my paw.

I'll destoy your beads and scapular,
    I'll worry dirty Joe ;
I'll chase your priests from Ireland,
    And expose your holy show.
I'll stop your nun's vile slavery,
    Your offspring I'll scrape up,
And expose your priest's iniquity ;
    Get off you Popish pup.

John's cur then gave a yelping sign,
    (Now Redmond's cur was a bitch),
And out sprang fifty Fenian dogs,
    From hiding in a ditch ;
But Carson's dog was ready,
    And tore them every one ;
And a bulldog that was watching,
    Cried, "Wash your mouth when you've done"

The bulldog now had started,
    To stop him none would try ;
He worried every Romish thing,
    And made the Fenians fly.
He restored the stolen children
    And made M'Cann repent ;
He destroyed the chapel wafers,
    The candles and the scent.

Copyright

114. Right - Donald Magill was a
very successful postcard illustrator
who used many topics as inspiration
for his art. This postcard was
published by Joseph Asher,
London.

119. Below - Ulster's determination
to remain part of the Union and to
have nothing to do with Home Rule
is strikingly depicted in this card
published by Johnson, Belfast.

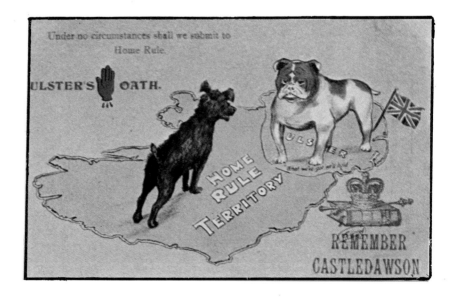

HOME RULE

YOU CAN LEAD A HORSE
TO THE WATER — BUT

·HOME·RULE·

" AN
ACT OF UNION "
WHICH SATISFIES BOTH
PARTIES.

Donald McGill.

118. Above - This postcard,
published by Valentine, Dublin,
shows Ulster's determination not to
accept Asquith's Home Rule Bill.

115. Left - Magill was a master of
the double-entendre and was most
at home in this genre. For the time
in which it was published, this card
seems a little risqué.

Carson's  Orange Cat.

Sir Edward Carson has a Cat,
    It sits upon the fender
And every time a mouse it gets,
    It shouts out No Surrender.

He left it by the fireside,
    When'er he went away
On his return he always found,
    It singing " Dollys Brae."

The Traitors grew indignant,
    At hearing such a noise
But Carson made the Cat sit up,
    And sing the " Protestant Boys."

The Traitors then decided
    To hang it with a rope
But every time they tried the rope,
    It yelled H—ll Roast the Pope.

The people came from far and near,
    To hear the Pussey sing
Good old Brittania Rules the Waves,
    And may " God Save the King."

A few said what a pity,
    The Cat is such a fool
But Carson's Cat yelled out the more,
    We will not have Home Rule.

122. Above - Verse was a favourite medium in which to castigate the concept of Home Rule at the time. This card cannot be attributed to any publisher.

123. Right - 'Ulster is armed to the teeth' - No. 15 in the Historic Events Series - poked fun at Ulster's determination to fight (before it had been armed) to preserve the Union.

HISTORIC EVENTS SERIES **"ULSTER IS ARMED TO THE TEETH."** [No. 15

There's Tammas McClusky and Betsy his wife,   And the childre they've reared, down to Samuel the wain.
Baith airmed to the teeth and baith ready for strife;   Bluidy wark will be done if this army's let fecht,
And their son William John and his wuman Ann Jane.   For Lord Randolph yince said it, "Their cause is the richt."

words of the verse 'Men, keep your Rifles free from Rust!' spell out all the dangers of the proposed bill and also the means to be employed by Ulstermen to defeat that bill (117). The feeling was widespread throughout Ulster that Asquith, the British prime minister, would listen to the counsel of John Redmond the leader of the Irish Parliamentary Party, whose votes he needed to stay in power, rather than to those of Carson. Much sly fun was poked at them, with neither Asquith nor Redmond being spared the jibe that no matter what they decided Ulster would block the way (118).

Carson's intransigent opposition to Home Rule was a fruitful theme for the postcard illustrator (119). 'Home Rule Territory', illustrated by G. Lemon and published by Johnson, depicts Carson as a fine example of the British bulldog breed which had carved out and still held a vast empire. This analogy is repeated in the versified postcard 'Sir Edward Carson's Bulldog "Ulster" ', and again in the card 'Home Rule Rout' illustrated by W. Watson and published by the Ulster Publishing Company (120, 121). It is changed slightly in the card 'Carson's Orange Cat' (122).

Carson's citizen army, the Ulster Volunteer Force, was founded early in 1913 and drilled openly throughout Ulster during the next year and a half. Despite the belligerent tone of

SEARCHING FOR ARMS IN ULSTER.

Bad luck to this huntin' for rifles, | There's M'Carty the dovecot inspectin',
And searchin' for other such loot ; | Where there's nothin' at all but stale eggs
We've bin huntin' all day for such trifles, | And Murphy, our pride at detectin',
And swallowin' mouthfuls av soot. | Houldin' on to the tree by his legs.

And O'Brien the windlass is windin',
To drop Mickey Toole in the well—
Historic Events Och, this searchin' for arms is like mindin'
Series The fires that are flamin' in——!

[*No. 11*

124. After the Larne gun-running the humorists turned their attention to the efforts of the RIC to find the smuggled arms.

the speeches of the Ulster leaders, public opinion tended to treat the notion of an unarmed army with derision. This is demonstrated by the postcard 'Ulster is Armed to the Teeth', No. 15 in the Historic Events Series (123).

However, the situation was changed after the night of 24 April 1914, when rifles and ammunition were landed at Larne, Bangor and Donaghadee. The resourcefulness of the volunteers in concealing their arms led to many good stories, some of which are still current in Ulster's folk mythology today (124-126).

SEARCHING FOR ARMS IN ULSTER.

They're howldin' on to Murphy, who thinks he's found a gun,
While O'Flanigan is divin' through a winda' at the run,
And Constable O'Hooligan inspects the chimney pot ;
But divil a wan av all av them a popgun, sure, has got.

Historic Events Series]   [*No. 12*

125. The antics of the search parties of the RIC looking for the smuggled
arms of the UVF are still part of Ulster's folklore.

In April 1918, at a very crucial stage of the European war,
the British government felt deep anxiety over the state of its
military reserves. A new Man-Power bill was hastily drafted
and debated, the main thrust of which called for the introduction of conscription. This bill would also apply to Ireland, and
immediately there was vigorous opposition from some Irish
members of the House of Commons. The idea of conscripting
Irishmen into the British army at such a difficult time in Anglo-
Irish affairs produced a spate of anti-conscription literature
and postcards (127, 128).

126. *Above* - Orange halls and Masonic lodges were searched in the attempt to locate the arms of the UVF. This postcard - No. 13 in the Historic Events Series - shows the dangers of searching Masonic lodges.

127. *Right* - Conscription in Ireland had always been a bone of contention between Nationalists and the British Government. This postcard - publisher unknown - pokes fun at even the concept.

128. *Page 122 top* - This card - No. 3 in a series - ridicules the lengths to which the recruiting sergeant will go to get conscripts.

129. *Page 122 bottom* - Social satire is used in this postcard, published by Socialists Unlimited, to attack the British government's economic and security policies and to show how the two combine.

THE FIRST IRISH CONSCRIPT.

The present 'troubles' have also brought forth political satirists among postcard illustrators. The marked difference between these and earlier illustrators is the consistently hard-hitting political point-scoring of the present generation. The continuing British presence in Northern Ireland is attacked in cards published by Socialists Unlimited of London. One makes the telling point that the troops that have to operate in riot situations in Ulster are working against their own class to help maintain the political, social and economic status quo in Britain – a status quo that forces boys and men to join the armed forces because of the high, and ever increasing, level of unemployment (129).

The Falkland crisis offered the republican movement an opportunity to reinforce its own *raison d'être*. The well-known republican cartoonist, Cormac, expressed the fundamental belief of the Provisional IRA in the last frame of his cartoon (see card 106).

The number of humorous political postcards produced during the present 'troubles' is low, mainly because of the depth of the tragedy which has scarred a generation, and will continue to scar future generations.

'Give 'em hell, lads. Remember you're fighting to preserve
the same kind of system that gave you no better choice than
to join the army and come out here and get shot at in the first place.'

APPENDIX A
ARTISTS AND ILLUSTRATORS

In the field of postcard production, the standard of illustrations was at a very high level between the years 1900 and 1920, many of the designs being the work of highly skilled and imaginative draftsmen and artists. Today, certain artists are collected for the excellence of their work or for their rarity value. Unfortunately most of the colourful political cards which have been dealt with already in this book are unsigned, and further research must be carried out to try to ascertain their designers. Most of the artists involved in illustrating Ulster political postcards were Ulstermen (notable exceptions are Ralph Cleaver and Donal McGill) and it is obvious that postcard illustration was not their sole, or even their main, occupation. For at least seven of the artists listed below, postcard illustration followed from magazine illustration and was really the reduction of an already published political cartoon to postcard size.

Campbell, John P. (1883-1962)

Campbell was a Belfastman (brother of the poet Joseph Campbell) who was much involved in the cultural life of his native city in the first decade of the twentieth century. He is well known as an illustrator of Celtic romances such as Mary Hutton's *The Táin* and C. Milligan Fox's *Four Irish Songs*. Much influenced by the Gaelic revival in the southern part of Ireland, Campbell took to signing his name in its Irish form: Seaghan Mac Cathmaoil or the abbreviated form S. McC. Around 1912 he emigrated to America where he continued to illustrate books, work in

the theatre and produce Irish pageants. All Campbell's postcards were published by the Dungannon Club, 114 Royal Avenue, who published the Sinn Féin newspaper *The Republic*. These cards were originally political cartoons which were reproduced as postcards and printed at the premises of *The Republic*. He had two cards published in this manner:

1 Ulster: The Parting of the Ways
2 Devolution Pie (see card 19).

As far as can be ascertained these are the only political cards illustrated by Campbell.

John P. Campbell

JOHN P. CAMPBELL
DIRECTOR I

Carey, John

John Carey, whose brother J. W. Carey (see below) also illustrated postcards, worked for such firms as Valentine, Baird, and Woolstone Bros. In general he drew romantic scenes from Irish life, favouring jaunting cars and courting couples. The only political card that he is known to have designed depicts a local Belfast politician, Mr Thomas H. Sloan, returning in triumph after retaining the south Belfast seat in the 1906 general election (130; see also card 8). Sloan is an interesting character. A shipyard worker, a temperance enthusiast and an evangelical preacher, he was expelled from the Orange Order for an act of insubordination against Colonel Saunderson, one of the staunchest of Unionists, but managed to elicit enough support to retain his seat in the ensuing election.

Carey, J. W. (1859-1937)

Joseph Carey, brother of John (above) was a painter of landscapes and seascapes. Son of the Rev. J. W. Carey, he received his early training in the firm of Marcus Ward and Co., Belfast, a firm highly regarded for the quality of its work. Joe, as he was affectionately known, illustrated postcards for Chas. L. Reis and Co., Dublin, and for the Ulidia Series. These cards depict the rural scenes of the time, such as turf cutting and linen bleaching; he dealt with Ireland's myths and legends in such cards as 'The landing of Deirdre and the sons of Usnach'. In 1906 he illustrated two political postcards for the Dungannon Club, Belfast. These took as their theme the liberal and nationalist sentiments of the United Irishmen, depicting a scene from the Battle of Antrim (see card 15), and the opening of the Chapel of St Mary in 1784, the first Catholic chapel to be built in Belfast for over 250 years (131). Postcard illustration was only a minor part of Carey's artistic output.

Clafferty, Jack (*b.* 1947)

Born in Buncrana, Co. Donegal in 1947, Clafferty has lived in London since 1966 where he became a founder member of the Troops Out Movement. Since 1971 he has produced posters and graphics on Ireland, including the 'England attacking Ireland' symbol used on posters and badges in many countries. His illustrations have been used in *The Plough, The Irish Citizen, Troops Out, An Phoblacht,* and *Time Out,* and in pamphlets published by Information on Ireland. Four of his designs have been used to illustrate postcards published by Socialists Unlimited of London: (a) Until we are

J. W. Carey

all free. . . (b) A nation that enslaves. . . (c) Britannia waives the rules. . . (d) If you don't know what's happening in Northern Ireland (see cards 101-105).

Cleaver, Ralph

An artist in black-and-white, Cleaver worked on many of the illustrated London papers in the 1890s, especially *The Graphic* and the *Daily Graphic* from 1906, specialising in naval and military subjects. He illustrated at least one card which was printed by David Allen and Sons Ltd., Harrow, Middlesex, and published by the National Unionist Association of Conservative and Liberal Unionists Organisations, St Stephen's Chambers, Westminster, S.W. It is entitled, 'Have you forgotten? Shall British troops be used against loyal Ulster?' and is the eighteenth card in a set (132). The card shows an angry Scots guardsman rejecting John Redmond's suggestion that Ulster should be coerced into accepting Home Rule by pointing to a poster which reads: 'British Disaster in South Africa cheered by Nationalist M.P.'. This card was printed at the time of the Curragh Mutiny in 1914.

William Conor

Conor, William (1881-1968)

William Conor was born on 6 May 1881 and attended Cliftonpark Central National School, Avoca Street, followed by the Government School of Design, after which he became an apprentice poster designer at David Allen and Son Ltd. During the First World War he was appointed by the government to paint official records of soldiers and munition workers. His paintings are of a very high quality and lend themselves to reproduction as postcards. His 'Charge of the Ulster Division' at Thiepval (see card 5), 1 July 1916, is characteristic of his work at this time. This card was published by the Headquarters Council Ulster Volunteer Force, Old Town Hall, and the proceeds of sale were devoted to the UVF Hospital for Sick and Wounded Soldiers and Sailors. Conor did much good work in aid of the hospital, designing cards and calendars for them. His first love was, and always remained, figure and portrait painting. He died on 5 February 1968 at his home, 107 Salisbury Avenue, Belfast, and was buried at Carnmoney churchyard.

Cormac

Cormac is a well-known and increasingly popular radical cartoonist. Born in north Belfast, he began his career as an illustrator with the Zany People's magazine *Resistance Comix*. He has contributed regularly to such papers as the *Andersonstown News, Republican News, An Phoblacht*, and has a weekly sketch in *Socialist Challenge*. In November 1982 Information on Ireland published a book of his collected cartoons, *Cormac Strikes Back* (133; see also card 106). He is also a competent musician.

Greer, A.

Greer resided at 24 Queen Street, Belfast. He was a magazine illustrator working chiefly on the *Belfast Weekly News*, on *Nomad's Weekly* and the *Belfast Critic*. During the turbulent years 1912-14 Greer's pencil sketches caricatured local dignitaries such as the lord mayor, attacked government policies towards Ireland and castigated John Redmond and the concept of Home Rule (134). These cartoons lent themselves readily to reproduction as postcards and were published as such by local firms, especially J. W. Patton, 106 North Street, Belfast.

Gunn, Bill

I have been unable to trace any biographical information concerning this artist. He illustrated only one card that has survived, 'Tax Collector John and Sir Edward', published by the Ulster Publishing Co., 20 Rosemary Street, Belfast (135). 'Bill Gunn' is almost certainly a pseudonym.

J.P.G.

A set of anti-Home Rule cards was published by the Ulster Publishing Co., 20 Rosemary Street, Belfast, designed by an artist signing himself or herself as J.P.G. Unfortunately, research has been unable to throw any light on the real name of the artist. However, J.P.G. was a poet as well as an artist and wrote verse to accompany the illustrations (136). To accompany the card 'West Belfast: Devlin's reserve voter's Depot: Joe's last call' he wrote 'Election Resurrection', which begins with the lines:

My name is Barney Murphy
In a Milltown grave I lie . . .

These cards and poems were reproduced in booklet form by the Ulster Publishing Co. and from this we learn that J.P.G. wrote seven poems to accompany artistic work.

J.V.B.

An artist, signing his or her work only with the initials J.V.B., designed cards for J. Johnson, 24 William Street, Belfast, and William Strain and Sons Ltd., Belfast. These cards are of high artistic quality, colourful and emotive, and have as their theme Ulster's determination to remain part of the empire and to resist Home Rule with force if necessary (138). No biographical details could be traced.

Kennard, Peter (*b.* 1949)

Kennard was born in London in 1949 and studied at the Byam Shaw School of Art and at the Slade. He moved from photography to work using a combination of paint and photography. He has lectured on art and politics for the

Workers' Educational Association and took a master of arts degree in fine art at the Royal College of Art. He has held many individual as well as mixed exhibitions in England and Australia, and his work is represented in many museums and universities. He has produced a set of six postcards using photomontage, one of which depicts sensory deprivation in Northern Ireland (1978). (See card 89.)

Lemon, George

The Belfast Street Directory for 1912 states that G. A. Lemon lived at 98 Donegall Street. Lemon was an artist-designer who provided illustrations for local magazines such as *Belfast Town Topics*, *Nomad's Weekly*, and *The Irish Tatler*. In the first issue of *The Irish Tatler*, 8 April 1911, he advertised his ability as a designer, sketcher, cartoonist and showcard illustrator. Lemon's illustrations were used by the firm of Johnson, 24 William Street, Belfast, who published 'Stand Back Redmond' (see card 113), a card which states emphatically 'your [Home Rule] bill may pass parliament, but it will not pass Ulster', and 'Home Rule Territory' (see card 119) which shows Ulster's bulldog spirit defending its territory against the Home Rule mongrel. Two other cards, not attributable to any publisher, depict rowdyism among local councillors in contention over the seat for North Belfast and the imminent struggle to maintain the link with Britain having precedents in Ulster's history.

George Lemon's card and self-portrait.

Lynd, Robert (1879-1949)

Robert Lynd was born in Belfast on 20 April 1879, the son of a Presbyterian minister. He was educated at Belfast Royal Academic Institution and Queen's College, Belfast. He contributed a number of sketches to the London *Outlook* while living in Belfast

Robert Lynd

national Art Company, as well as Eyre and Spottiswood. He is best known for his colourful seaside scenes whose captions shocked many a 'maiden aunt'. Magill illustrated literally thousands of cards using many themes, one of which was Home Rule for Ireland. Three cards he illustrated for Joseph Asher & Co., 3-4 Ivy Lane, London E.C., are in his unmistakeable comic style. One shows 'Pat' being attacked by his wife, and bears the caption: 'Phwat! You talk about being a Home Ruler whoile oi'm aloive!!'

Another shows an Irish lad and lass drawn with a heart and in the act of kissing; the caption reads: 'An Act of Union, which satisfies both parties' (see card 115 and cover). This *double entendre* was a trade-mark of Magill's, and for the time was *risqué* in the extreme.

The third card is entitled 'Home Rule – An Orangeman in Ulster' (see card 114).

and, in 1901, obtained a temporary post as descriptive writer on the Manchester *Daily Despatch*. He contributed regularly to the *New Statesman*, chiefly essays bearing the signature 'Y.Y.' Lynd favoured national self-determination for Ireland, and was a leading member of the London Gaelic League. He contributed articles and cartoons to the Belfast Sinn Féin newspaper *The Republic* and two of these cartoons were reproduced as postcards; they cast ridicule on the Irish party's willingness to bargain for Home Rule in the British Parliament (see card 20).

Magill, Donald

Donald Magill died in the early 1960s after one of the most successful careers as a postcard illustrator. He illustrated cards for Joseph Asher & Co., the Inter-

Morrow, E. A. (*b*. 1877)

Edwin Morrow, born in 1877, was a member of an artistic and literary Belfast family. He attended the School of Design, Belfast, and won a scholarship to the South Kensington School of Art, becoming a portrait and landscape painter, and black-and-white artist. He is known to have illustrated only one political postcard, 'The Undying Oath', published by the Dungannon Club.

Morrow, George (1870-1955)

George Morrow was the best-known artist in a family of artists and painters. He attended the School of Design, Belfast, and exhibited later at the Royal Academy and the Royal Society of British Artists. In 1906 he began to contribute to *Punch* and having contributed for some eighteen years he joined the staff in 1924, and became art editor in 1932. Also in 1906 he was contributing to *The Republic* – a less well-known but more revolutionary paper in his native city. A political cartoon drawn by George Morrow and published in *The Republic* on 27 December 1906 was reproduced as a postcard (see card 17). In style it seems to have been influenced by the drawings of John P. Campbell. This is the only drawing by George Morrow which is known to have been reproduced as a postcard.

Morrow, Jack (1872-1926)

Jack Morrow was intimately involved in the early days of the Ulster Literary Theatre. A landscape painter and a political cartoonist, Jack Morrow was the most politically active of the Morrow brothers. He contributed pictures and cartoons to *The Republic, The Irish Review* and other contemporary Irish journals. He was acknowledged as the most promising of his fellow young Irish artists, his work showing not only promise but power. His political cartoon 'The Secret of England's Greatness', published in *The Republic*, 17 January 1907, was reproduced as a postcard and published by the Dungannon Club (see card 16). It is his only known card.

Morrow, Norman (1879-1927)

Norman Morrow was also intimately involved in the early days of the Ulster Literary Theatre, designing sets, acting and managing. He was a member of the Belfast Art Society and exhibited regularly at their annual exhibitions. Only one political postcard is known to have been designed by him, 'Sinn Féin and Prosperity', which appeared as a cartoon in *The Republic*, 24 January 1907, and was published as a card by the Dungannon Club (see card 21).

S.H.Y.

This artist, signing as S.H.Y., worked for the firm of Valentine, of Dundee and Dublin. The cards, black-and-white illustrations, are satirical attacks on Carson's often-stated threat to detach Ulster from any scheme of Home Rule for Ulster (138). No biographical details have been traced.

Spengler, Christine

Spengler is a distinguished freelance French photographer who has covered many of the world's trouble-spots, including Vietnam, Cyprus, Portugal and Northern Ireland. Her work has appeared extensively in *Life, Time, Newsweek* and *Paris Match*. Principally a photographer, she has from time to time published her work in postcard form. She has over four thousand negatives of Northern Ireland on file and from these she selected fifteen for her postcard series, printed in Belfast (see cards 82-87).

Watson, William

Watson illustrated political postcards for W. & G. Baird Ltd., Belfast, J. Johnson, 24 William Street, Belfast, The Ulster Publishing Co., and for at least one other local firm, possibly H. Courtney, Anne Street, Belfast. His illustrations are usually black-and-white, humorous and anti-Home Rule. His most impressive work was done for the Ulster Publishing Co., who published a set of postcards of high artistic merit (see card 121). As well as being an artist, Watson was something of a poet, and published a poem entitled 'Ulster's Reward' in *The Times* of 14 September 1912, which was reproduced as a postcard.

APPENDIX B
PUBLISHERS OF
ULSTER POLITICAL POSTCARDS

Below is a list of as many publishers of
Ulster political postcards as have been
traced by the author, along with the
titles of their cards. In the case of
commercial publishers between 1905
and 1985, the address of the firm and a
detailed description – if available – of
their general function have been given.
In the case of election postcards
published between 1968 and 1985, these
have been arranged under the name of
the political party and not the name of
the publisher (usually the candidate's
election agent) as this was felt to be
more useful to the reader. Most of the
1968-85 election postcards mentioned
below are in the possession of the Linen
Hall Library; many more were
published, but few have survived or
have been collected. Many postcards
dealing with political events in Ulster
between 1905 and 1985 cannot be attributed to a specific publisher and are
therefore not mentioned in this bibliography. The Sinn Féin rebellion of 1916
is treated in Appendix E since, although
it falls outside the general scope of this
book, it was affected by – and later
affected – events in Ulster. A short
bibliography of postcards related to
1916 is appended to the text of Appendix E as it was felt that to include them
in this bibliography of Ulster political
postcards would be confusing to the
reader.

ADAMS, John, 39-43 New King Street,
Belfast. Artistic letterpress printer,
bookbinder and stationer.

cards
  1 Ulster's Question – Under which flag?
  2 We won't have Home Rule (inset picture

of Carson) (card 45)
  3 We won't have Home Rule (inset picture
    of Ulster Unionist Council Headquar-
    ters)
  4 We won't have Home Rule (inset of
    William Moore K.C.) (card 44)
  5 We won't have Home Rule (inset of
    Capt. James Craig)
  6 We won't have Home Rule (inset of
    Charles Craig M.P.) (card 46)

ALLIANCE PARTY
cards
Oliver Napier; European election, 7 June
  1979
Bob Cooper; Convention election, 1 May
  1975
David Cooke; Westminster election, 9 June
  1983
Oliver Napier; Westminster election, 3 May
  1979
Joan Tomlin / Gordon Mawhinney /
  Seamus Close; Assembly election, 20
  October 1982
John Cushnahan / Lord Dunleath / Brian
  Wilson; Assembly election, 20 October
  1982
Paddy Morrow / Oliver Napier; Assembly
  election, 20 October 1982
Will Glendenning; Assembly election, 20
  October 1982
David Cooke; Westminster election, 4
  March 1982
Paul Maguire; Assembly Election, 20
  October 1982
Basil Glass / Jim Hendron; Convention
  election, 1 May 1975
Muriel Pritchard / Bill Jeffery / David
  Cooke; Belfast City Council election, 20
  May 1984
Oliver Napier; Westminster election, 9 June
  1983
David Cooke; Executive election, 28
  February 1974
Lord Dunleath / Keith Jones / Bertie
  McConnell; Convention election, 1 May
  1975

Triumphant Return of Mr. Sloan, M.P., and his Backers after winning the Parliamentary Handicap with Independent Unionism (by Integrity out of Protestantism).

130. John Carey was adept at producing romantic illustrations of Irish life. Sloan's victory gave him great scope to portray his sentiments in postcard form.

Michael Brown / Oliver Napier / David Wonnacott; Belfast City Council Election, n.d.

Basil Glass; Westminster election, 3 May 1979

John Cushnahan; Westminster election, 9 June 1983

Paul Maguire; Westminster election, 9 June 1983

ASHER, JOSEPH & CO.,
3-4 Ivy Lane, London E.C.

cards
1 Home Rule – An act of union which satisfies both parties (card 115)
2 Home Rule (card 114)

BAIRD, W. & G. LTD.,
124-132 Royal Avenue, Belfast. Letterpress and lithographic printers, bookbinders, account book manufacturers, wholesale stationers, photo process engravers and electrotypers.

cards
1 Mr Churchill leaving Grand Central Hotel, Belfast, for Celtic Park Meeting
2 Donegall Place, Belfast, under Home Rule
3 One crown, one Parliament, one flag
4 UVF motorcycle column
5 Ulster at bay as in 1690 and *now*
6 Carson rejecting skull (Home Rule) from Redmond
7 Belfast under Home Rule
8 To Mr Asquith
9 UVF training ground
10 Which way shall you drive him?
11 Home Rule Parliament, College Green 1915. Discussing the Military Defences of the Kingdom
12 Councillor Dr Henry O'Neill (Conservative and Unionist Candidate for South Belfast, 1905)
13 Inspection by Sir E. Carson, Ballykinlar Camp
14 The late Colonel Saunderson M.P.

BOYD, J. W. & CO.,
44-46 North Street, Belfast. Printer.

cards
1 Belfast Strike – The first incident: Lamp uprooted in Waring Street (card 23)
2 Belfast Strike – Lorry overturned by Strikers in Gt. George's Street
3 Belfast Strike – Motor waggon and police escort in Donegall Street
4 Belfast Strike – Ex-constable Barrett chaired by his admirers (card 31)
5 Belfast Strike – Military cooks at work in Ormeau Park
6 Belfast Strike – Scene in Queen's Square (card 35)
7 Belfast Strike – Military on Guard at Donegall Quay
8 Belfast Strike – Van of paper overturned in Great George's Street
9 Belfast Strike – Conveying goods to the Quay under police protection (card 29)
10 Belfast Strike – Maxim gun section of the Middlesex Regiment in Ormeau Park
11 Belfast Strike – Military Guard at Custom House, Donegall Quay
12 Charles McMullan – One of the victims shot in Belfast riots on Monday August 12th 1907
13 Funeral of Charles McMullan and Margaret Lennon, victims of Belfast riots
14 Funeral victims, Belfast Riots at Leeson Street (card 32)

BROWN, JAS., Limavady. Newsagent.

cards
1 UVF demonstration, Limavady, 16th April, 1914
2 UVF demonstration, Limavady, 16th April, 1914 (street scene)
3 UVF demonstration, Limavady, 16th April, 1914 (Catherine St.)
4 UVF demonstration, Limavady, 16th April, 1914 (Review of UVF troop)

BROWN, WM. & SON,
30 Chichester Street, Belfast. Printers and Stationers.

cards
1 Ulster's Solemn Covenant 1912

CANNING, Bankmore Street, Belfast.

cards
1 Ulster's ABC

CARTER, A. J.,
Terminus Road, Eastbourne.

cards
1 Lloyd George's favourite dinner

CARTER, H. R.,
28-36 Waring Street, Belfast.

cards
1 We will not have Home Rule
2 Ulster will fight and Ulster will be right
3 Government seizure of arms at Belfast Quay
4 Sir Edward Carson: 'My place is in Ireland'

THE OLD CHAPEL OF SAINT MARY, BELFAST, 30TH MAY, 1784.

The first Catholic Chapel built in Belfast for over two hundred and fifty years. The Volunteers attended the ceremony in full uniform; the patriotic Protestants filled the building and subscribed most of the funds for its erection.

" We anxiously wish to see the day when every Irishman shall be a citizen, when Catholics and Protestants, equally interested in their country's welfare, possessing equal freedom and equal privileges, shall be cordially UNITED, and shall learn to look upon each other as brethren, the children of the same God, the natives of the same land, and when the only strife amongst them shall be—who shall serve their country best."

Address from the Protestant Patriots of Belfast in 1792.

Dungannon Club Series.   Printed in Ireland.

131. J. W. Carey drew his inspiration from the heroic in Irish life. He drew many fine illustrations with the National Volunteers as theme. This postcard, published by the Dungannon Club, shows the Belfast Volunteers providing a guard of honour at the opening of St. Mary's Roman Catholic Church, Belfast.

 5 Reception of Sir Edward by his troops
 6 Volunteer squad seeking to gain cover
 7 Retreating to take up a fresh position
 8 Volunteers storming a hill
 9 Ulster women do what they can
10 Typical Ulster Volunteer
11 Principal members of Ulster Provisional Government
12 Ulster's Solemn League and Covenant
13 Bravo! Ulster Volunteers
14 Ulster 1914. Deserted! Well I can stand alone
15 The plot that failed
16 The plot that did not fail
17 Ulster Volunteers flying squad
18 South Belfast Regiment
19 Grand Review at Balmoral
20 Saviours of Ulster
21 Sir Edward Carson
22 Ulster Covenant
23 Sir Edward Carson Reviewing his troops
24 Ulster Volunteer Review at Antrim
25 Ulster Horse at Clandeboye
26 Review at Clandeboye

CHARLES and RUSSELL,
10 Royal Avenue, Belfast. Photographers.

cards
  1 Carson signing the Solemn League and
    Covenant

CLELAND, JOHN AND SON LTD.,
68-70 Great Victoria Street, Belfast.
Fancy box makers, mercantile stationers,
account book makers, letterpress printers,
lithographers, engravers, bookbinders and
embossers.

cards
  1 Loyal Ireland does not require or want
    Home Rule in any shape (card 47)
  2 Ulster's Prayer – don't let go
  3 No Home Rule (card 40)
  4 All round Home Rule – four square
    Home Rule – We want neither

CLELAND, WM. W. LTD.,
56 Great Victoria Street and Cullingtree
Factory, Belfast. Letterpress printers and
lithographers.

cards
  1 Ulster ever offers friendship . . . but
    when treacherous foes assail her

CORONA PUBLISHING CO.,
Blackpool

cards
  1 Who says we'll have Home Rule (card
    48)

COURTNEY, H., Anne Street, Belfast.
Printer.

cards
  1 Ulster's Reward
  2 Ulster's Appeal

DEMOCRATIC UNIONIST
LOYALIST COALITION

cards
Tommy Wright; Assembly election, 28
  June 1973
T. E. Burns; Assembly election, 28 June
  1973

Eileen E. Paisley; Assembly election, 28
  June 1973 (card 79)
Charles Poots; Assembly election, 28 June
  1973

DEMOCRATIC UNIONIST PARTY
cards
George Seawright; Westminster election, 9
  June 1983
Peter Robinson; Westminster election, 9
  June 1983

DESIGN 4, Newtownards, N. Ireland.

cards
  1 Wedding Guests, North Belfast 1973
  2 Sandy Row, Belfast, 1974
  3 Sandy Row, Belfast, 1974
  4 'The Field', Irvinestown,
    Co. Fermanagh, 1975
  5 Donegall Square, Belfast, 1975
  6 Royal Avenue, Belfast, 1975
  7 York Street, Belfast, 1975
  8 Belfast City Hall, 1975

DUNGANNON CLUB, The,
114 Royal Avenue Belfast.

cards
  1 The Battle of Antrim, 7th June, 1798
    (card 15)
  2 The Old Chapel of St. Mary, Belfast
    30th May, 1784 (card 131)
  3 Catching Recruits (card 10)
  4 The Stranger in the House (card 17)
  5 The Secret of England's Greatness (card
    16)
  6 Sinn Féin and Prosperity (card 21)
  7 The Wild Geese, 1907 (card 18)
  8 Devolution Pie (card 19)
  9 Ulster: The Parting of the Ways
  10 John Bull's Famous Circus (card 20)
  11 Irish Anti-National Exhibition
  12 John Bull and Sinn Féin
  13 Portrait of the Dead Fenian, John
    O'Leary
  14 The Undying Oath
  15 The National Volunteers in College
    Green, Dublin (card 12)
  16 The Irish House of Commons during
    the War of Independence 1782-1800
    (card 13)
  17 The Battle of Ballynahinch (card 14)

No 18 P.C.

HAVE   YOU   FORGOTTEN ?

BRITISH DISASTER IN SOUTH AFRICA CHEERED BY NATIONALIST MPs

**SHALL BRITISH TROOPS BE USED
AGAINST LOYAL ULSTER ?**

132. Ulster's decision to fight Home Rule - and to form an independent state, if necessary - would almost certainly mean armed intervention by the British Government. Ralph Cleaver illustrates the dilemma in a postcard published by the National Unionist Association of Conservative and Liberal Unionist Organisations.

EXCHANGE PUBLISHING CO.,
36 Shankill Road, Belfast.

cards
  1 Sir Edward, My Boy
  2 Men keep your rifles free from rust (card
     117)
  3 They can't bell Carson's cart
  4 Carson's Orange Parrot
  5 The Political ABC
  6 The Roll of honoured dead
  7 Saviours of Ulster
  8 A fight to the finish

FAULKNER, C. W. LTD., London.

card
  1 The Ulster Covenant

GLEN PHOTOGRAPHY, Dundalk.

cards

  1 Boucher Gate, Derry
  2 You are now entering Free Derry
  3 Roaring Meg
  4 Loyalist decorations in Fountain Street,
     Derry

GRAHAM AND HESLIP,
11 Franklin Street, Belfast.

card
   1 How East Down was wooed
     But not won by Wood

GRAHAM GLEN, H. Wortley Ltd.,
Leeds.

card
   1 Shut the gates again

HALLIDAY, C. H.,
Royal Avenue, Belfast.

card
   1 Edward Carson (card 9)

HENDERSON'S LTD.,
Newtownstewart.

cards
   1 UVF Camp, Baronscourt, 1913
   2 UVF Camp, Baronscourt, 1913

HISTORIC EVENTS SERIES

cards
Bravo, Ulster!
   1 (Untraced)
   2 The track of the Gun Runners at Larne,
     as seen from Islandmagee
   3 The Gun Runners on the road to Belfast
     from Larne
   4 (Untraced)
   5 Unloading the guns at Bangor Pier
   6 Unloading the guns at Donaghadee
   7 Waiting for the guns at Bangor, 24th
     April, 1914
   8 Searching for arms in Ulster (card 124)
   9 Searching for arms in Ulster (card 125)
   10 Searching for arms in Ulster (card 66)
   11 Searching for arms in Ulster (card 126)
   12 Searching for arms in Ulster (card 67)
   13 Orange Proclamation
   14 The New Map
   15 Ulster is armed to the teeth (card 123)
   16 No Surrender!
   17 A rude Irish blackthorn
   18 The Red Hand of Ulster
   19 Keeping the pot boiling in Ireland
   20 The Ulster Volunteers protecting a
      Sunday School excursion in Ulster
   21 Edward of Ulster crossing the Boyne

HURST & CO., Fine Art Warehouse,
Corn Market, Belfast. Printsellers, picture
frame makers, gilders, fancy and leather
goods dealers, artists' colourmen.

cards
   1 Ulster Day – Sir Edward Carson signing
     the Covenant (card 55)
   2 Unionist demonstration at Belfast 9th
     April, 1912 – breaking the monster
     Union Jack
   3 The Rt. Hon. Andrew Bonar Law, M.P.
     photographed at Mountstewart 9th
     April, 1912
   4 Sir E. Carson leaving Belfast for Ennis-
     killen to open Ulster Day Campaign.
   5 Sir E. Carson and the Irish Unionist
     Parliamentary Party
   6 Belfast Citizens assembled outside City
     Hall to sign Covenant 28th September,
     1912
   7 Unionist clubs entering City Hall to sign
     Covenant – Ulster Day 28th September,
     1912
   8 Outside Ulster Hall on eve of Ulster
     Day after presentation of the Orange
     flag to Sir E. Carson, 27th September,
     1912
   9 Belfast Streets on Ulster Day 28th
     September, 1912
   10 Audience at Ulster Hall meeting,
      addressed by Sir E. Carson and other
      prominent leaders, on Ulster Day eve,
      27th September, 1912
   11 The speakers and view of the Ulster Hall
      platform on eve of Ulster Day, 27th
      September, 1912
   12 Ulster Unionist delegates ratifying
      Covenant in Ulster Hall Belfast, 23rd
      September, 1912
   13 UVF – South Belfast Regiment en route
      for Balmoral, 27th September, 1913
      (card 59)
   14 UVF – Flying squadron at Balmoral, 27th
      September, 1913
   15 Sir E. Carson and Lady Carson, General
      and Lady Richardson witnessing review
      of the Ulster Division, Kitchener's
      army, at Belfast, 8th May, 1915

134. Above - The ship of Home Rule foundering on the Rock of Ulster is the clever theme of this card published by W. J. Patton, Belfast.

135. Below - Carson's determined fight against Home Rule and his reasons for that fight are humorously shown in this postcard published by the Ulster Publishing Co., Belfast.

16 Sir Edward and Lady Carson
17 Sir E. Carson's bodyguard at religious service in courtyard, City Hall, Ulster Day
18 South Belfast Regiment, UVF, passing saluting base, Balmoral Review, 6th June, 1914
19 The Great Review at Balmoral, 27th September, 1913 – A general view showing some of the troops (card 60)
20 The Sandy Row Volunteers drawn up ready to march to Balmoral, 27th September, 1913
21 Sir E. Carson inspecting the young citizen volunteers at Balmoral, 6th June, 1914
22 Balmoral Review, 27th September, 1913, – General Richardson giving instructions to his galloper F. E. Smith, K.C.
23 Sir E. Carson acknowledging the cheers of UVF at Glencuim, 6th June, 1914
24 Sir E. Carson and Col. Wallace
25 Bravo! Ulster Volunteers – 'Hands across the sea . . .'
26 Bravo! Ulster Volunteers – 'They think to send you Tommy . . .'
27 Bravo! Ulster Volunteers – 'When Asquith, quite polite like . . .'
28 Inspection of 12,000 men of the Belfast Division UVF (card 58)
29 'I rely on every man to fight'
30 Sir Edward Carson, K.C., M.P.
31 Ulster Division, Ambulance Section, Kitchener's Army, passing through Donegall Square North, 8th May, 1915
32 Ulster Division, Kitchener's Army. Col. Wallace, Col. Sharman-Crawford, Capt. Barnett, and brother officers at Review in Belfast, 8th May, 1915
33 Ulster Division, Kitchener's Army. Officers of the YCV approaching saluting point on parade at Belfast, 8th May, 1915
34 Review of Ulster Division, Kitchener's Army, at Belfast, 8th May, 1915. The Procession passing the saluting base.
35 Review of Ulster Division, Kitchener's Army, at Belfast, 8th May, 1915. The Irish Fusiliers passing through Chichester Street
36 Platform at Women's Anti-Home Rule Demonstration in Ulster Hall, 30th September, 1912
37 Audience at Women's Anti-Home Rule Demonstration in Ulster Hall, 30th September, 1912
38 View of platform, Ulster Business Men's Protest Meeting against Home Rule, 4th November, 1913
39 UVF Fortwilliam section North Belfast Regiment starting for Balmoral, 27th September, 1913
40 The headquarters of the Ulster Unionist Council and Unionist Clubs of Ireland

INDEPENDENT

cards
Bernadette Devlin; EEC election, 7 June 1979
Moya Saunders; local council election, 30 May 1973
Joe Rigby; local council election, 30 May 1973
Rory McShane; Assembly election, 28 June 1973
Jim Kilfedder; Westminster election, 9 June 1983

INDEPENDENT LABOUR

card
Raymond Heath; n.d.

JEFFERS, Postcard Publishers, Portadown.

card
1 St. Mark's Church and Colonel Saunderson's Statue, Portadown

JOHNSTON, JAMES,
24 William Street South, Belfast. Photographer, stationer, publisher and importer.

cards
1 Ulster 1914 (card 70)
2 How is freedom measured
3 No Home Rule
4 Ulster 1914 deserted
5 Ulster to England (card 137)
6 Stand back Redmond (card 113)
7 Armed parade of the young citizen battalion, Ulster Volunteers

133. *Above* - Women's rights is a concept much talked about by Irish men but seldom actively supported. Cormac epitomizes the general attitude in this postcard published by the Republican movement.

136. *Below* -Personation - the unlawful use of another's vote - has bedevilled Ulster politics for eight decades. In this card, published by the Ulster Publishing Co., the illustrator shows Joseph Devlin carry it to extreme lengths.

8 Ulster's leader – Lieut. Col. Sir James Craig (card 50)
9 C. Company young citizen Volunteers in dress uniform
10 Ulster Volunteer Force Hospital – The wounded soldiers
11 The Orange Order
12 Ulster's Solemn Covenant we will maintain
13 Home Rule Territory (card 119)
14 Parade passing Mulholland's Nursery Gardens, Lisburn Rd.
15 Twelfth of July march. *c.* 1910
16 King William III, crossing the Boyne, July 1st, 1690

JUST BOOKS, Winetavern Street, Belfast.
cards
1 Greetings from Northern Ireland: Until all are free we are all imprisoned
2 Greetings from Northern Ireland: Get the Brits out
3 Michael McCartan was murdered
4 Keeping the peace
5 Returning the empties
6 'They murder the innocent in vengeance . . .'
7 On a clear day you can see the revolution from here
8 Civil Order
9 Wall Mural in Moira Street, Short Strand, Belfast (card 107)
10 1984 International Women's Day Picket outside Armagh Jail (card 112)
11 Untitled. (Riot Scene) (card 108)
12 Untitled. (Soldiers aiming plastic batton rounds) (card 111)
13 Our Day will Come
14 Afternoon Class in Motor Maintenance: Week 3 'The Exhaust System' (page 1)

KENNEDY, G., 50 York Street, Belfast.
card
1 Ulster Covenant Day 28th September, 1912 (card 56)

KNIGHT SERIES, The, (printed in England)
card
1 Colonel the Rt. Hon. E. J. Saunderson, M.P.

LAWRENCE PUBLISHERS, Dublin.
cards
1 The Relief of Derry
2 The Orange Hall, Belfast

LEEDS POSTCARDS,
13 Claremont Grove, Leeds L53 1AX
cards
1 Fighting to preserve the system
2 If you don't know what's happening in Northern Ireland . . .(card 104)
3 Ireland Shouts
4 Plastic Bullets: They smash heads (card 110)
5 Not fit to be used on humans: Plastic bullets

LITTLE LTD., London
cards
1 'So don't forget amigos, you can't be really "liberated" until you learn to laugh.'
2 Stone Walls do not a prison make, nor iron bars a cage . . .
3 'There was a young lady named Alice . . .'
4 I thought the Colt 45 was an American beer until I discovered Anarchy
5 When the going gets tough, the toughs get going
6 Prison? It's all mind over matter
7 Some days I just feel angry
8 I thought the M-16 was a motorway until I discovered Anarchy

LOYALIST COALITION
card
Michael Brooks; 30 May 1973

LYTTLE, R. CLEMENTS, 44 Dublin Road, Belfast.
Official Photographer to the Irish Football Association.
cards
1 UVF battalion
2 No Surrender
3 Untitled – UVF unit
4 Members of Ulster's first parliament opened in Belfast City Hall 7th June, 1921

137. Ulster's determination to remain part of the Union of Great Britain and Ireland is summed up in the lines of this card, published by J. Johnson, Belfast.

McCAW, STEVENSON and ORR (Marcus Ward Series).

card
1 The Orange Hall, Belfast

MACK, E., 104 King Henry's Road, London N.W.

card
1 Lloyd George's favourite dinner

MARTIN AND MURTRY, Belfast

card
1 Thomas H. Sloan, Esq., M.P. (Belfast South M.P. 1902-1910) (card 8)

MILLAR AND LANG, LTD., Art Publishers, Glasgow and London.

card
1 United we stand, divided we fall

MURRAY, RICHARDSON & CO., Dungannon.

card
1 Ulster Volunteer Drill Hall, Dungannon

NATIONAL UNIONIST Association of Conservative and Liberal Unionist Organisations

card
1 Have we forgotten? Shall British troops be used against loyal Ulster? (card 132)

NICHOLSON, John,
26 Church Lane, Belfast.
Printer and Stationer.

cards
1 Carson's Orange Cat
2 The Budget and Home Rule: or Mr. John Redmond appeals to Mr. Wm. O'Brien

'NO SURRENDER' SERIES
1 The Protestant boys shall carry the Drum
2 The Siege of Derry – from the painting by Contemporary Dutch artist Remeyn de Hooge
3 The Relief of Derry – The Mountjoy breaking the boom
4 The Apprentice Boys and No Surrender
5 William III Prince of Orange crossing the Boyne

NORTHERN IRELAND
LABOUR PARTY

cards
Erskine Holmes; Convention Election, 1 May 1975
Erskine Holmes; Westminster election, n.d.
Erskine Holmes; Assembly election, n.d.
Boyd; Westminster election, 1 May 1975
Norman Seawright; Westminster election, 20 October 1963
David Bleakley / Sandy Scott; Convention election, 1 May 1975
George Chambers; Westminster election, 3 May 1979

John Coulthard; Westminster election, 18 June 1969
Erskine Holmes; 18 June 1970
Paddy Devlin; Stormont election, 24 February, 1969 (card 75)
Alan Carr; Westminster election, 3 May 1979

OFFICIAL ULSTER UNIONIST

cards
Roy Bradford; Convention election, 1 May 1975 (card 88)
Robert Bradford; Westminster election, 3 May 1979

OFFICIAL UNIONIST PARTY
cards
Jim Kilfedder / George Green; Assembly election, 20 October 1982
John Taylor; European election, 1983
David McNarry; Assembly election, 20 October 1982
David McNarry; Assembly election, 28 June 1973
Stratton Mills; Stormont election, 18 June 1970 (card 78)
Rafton Pounder; Westminster election, 28 February 1974
Peter McLachlan; Westminster election, 10 October 1974
Ronald Broadhurst; Assembly election, 28 June 1973
Bill Martin; Assembly election, 28 June 1973
Brian Faulkner; Assembly election, 28 June 1973 (card 80)
Brian Faulkner; Stormont election, 24 February 1969
Denys Rowan-Hamilton; Stormont election, 24 February 1969
Dorothy Dunlop; Convention election, 29 May 1975
Jim Kilfedder; Assembly election, 28 June 1973
Bob McCartney; Westminster election, 9 June 1983
Jeremy Burchall; Westminster election, 9 June 1983
Cecil Walker; Westminster election, 9 June 1983
Jim Molyneaux; Westminster election, 3 May 1979

138. The consequences of Carson's insistence on the exclusion of Ulster from any implementation of Home Rule is graphically shown in this card published by Valentine, Dublin.

OFFICIAL UNITED UNIONIST PARTY

card
Robert Bradford; Westminster election, 10 October 1974

PATTON, W. J.,
106 North Street, Belfast.

card
1 Full steam Ahead (card 134)

PEOPLE'S DEMOCRACY

cards
1 April Fool Quiz
2 UDR Roll of Honour

PHOTOCROM CO. LTD.,
London and Tunbridge Wells.

cards
1 No Home Rule
2 Covenant day in Belfast (card 57)

PORTER, C. & CO., Belfast.

card
  1 Character of King William

'PRINTERIES', THE,
Gorton Lane, Manchester.

card
  1 A Grand Member's Concert will shortly
    be given in the House of Commons

PROTESTANT UNIONIST

card
John D. McKeague; Belfast City Council
  election, 12 February 1969

REPUBLICAN CLUBS

card
Noel Collins / Samuel Dowling / Edward
  O'Hagan; Assembly election

REPUBLICAN LABOUR PARTY

card
Paddy Kennedy; Assembly election, 28
  June 1974

REPUBLICAN MOVEMENT, The,
44 Parnell Square, Dublin.

cards
  1 Resistance
  2 The Proclamation of Poblacht na h-Éir-
    eann
  3 What's all this about liberation?
  4 Gunboat diplomacy (card 106)
  5 The British way of life in Ireland (card
    93)
  6 The British way of life in Ireland (card
    95)
  7 The British way of life in Ireland
  8 Revolutionary Greetings from Ireland
    (card 91)
  9 Revolutionary Greetings from Ireland
    (card 97)
 10 Revolutionary Greetings from Ireland
    (card 98)
 11 Revolutionary Greetings from Ireland
    (card 99)
 12 Revolutionary Greetings from Ireland
    (card 100)
 13 Revolutionary Greetings from Ireland
 14 H-Block Protesters
 15 Death Bullets (card 96)
 16 The film to end all films
 17 International Women's Day 1982 (card
    133)
 18 Fuair siad bás ar son na h-Éireann
 19 Countess Markievicz
 20 IRA volunteer Bobby Sands MP, aged
    27, from Belfast (card 94)
 21 INLA volunteer Micky Devine, aged 27,
    from Derry City
 22 IRA volunteer Thomas McElwee, aged
    23, from Bellaghy, South Derry
 23 IRA volunteer Kieran Doherty, aged 25,
    from Belfast
 24 INLA volunteer Kevin Lynch, aged 25,
    from Dungiven, North Derry
 25 IRA volunteer Martin Hurson, aged 24,
    from Cappagh, East Tyrone
 26 IRA volunteer Joe McDonnell, aged 30,
    from Belfast
 27 IRA volunteer Patsy O'Hara, aged 24,
    from Derry City
 28 IRA volunteer Raymond McCreesh,
    aged 24, from Carlough, South Armagh
 29 IRA volunteer Francis Hughes, aged 25,
    from Bellaghy, South Derry
 30 You are now entering Free Derry
 31 Mise Éire
 32 Stop the Armagh Strip searches

ROTARY PHOTOGRAPHIC SERIES,
London.

cards
  1 Principal members of the provisional
    government of Ulster
  2 One King, one flag, one fleet, one
    empire
  3 The Covenant

SIBBINS, A., Belfast.

card
  1 God save the King

SOCIAL DEMOCRATIC
AND LABOUR PARTY

cards

J. Clenaghan / J. McDonald / P. Ritchie; Assembly election, 20 October 1982

McCart / Milligan / Trainor; Newry & Mourne District Council election, 18 May 1977

Peter Prendiville; Westminster election, 9 June 1983

Denis Haughey; Westminster election, 9 June 1983

John Hume; European election, 1983 (card 90)

J. Goan / P. Tanney; Local Government election, 30 May 1973

Desmond Gillespie; Westminster election, 28 February 1974

William T. Annon; Assembly election, 28 June 1973

John Taylor; EEC election, 7 June 1979

Joe Hendron; Westminster election, 9 June 1983

Alistair McDonnell; Westminster election, 9 June 1983

Cathal O'Baoill; Westminster election, 9 June 1983

Brian Feeney; Westminster election, 9 June 1983

Sean Hollywood; Westminster election, 28 February 1974

SOCIALISTS UNLIMITED,
267 Seven Sisters Road, Finsbury Park, London N4 2DE.

cards

1 Until we are all free, we are all imprisoned (card 101)
2 Britannia waives the rules (card 103)
3 If you don't know what's happening in Northern Ireland you must have been watching British television, listening to British radio and reading the British Press (card 105)
4 A nation that enslaves another can never itself be free (card 102)
5 Fighting to preserve the system (card 129)

STIEBEL, ALFRED & CO., London.

cards

1 Home, Sweet Home Rule
2 Imperial Theatre, Westminster

STRAIN, WM. & SON,
21 and 60 Great Victoria Street, Belfast.

cards

1 Ulster's Solemn League and Covenant
2 Ulster 1914 (card 71)

TOLMERS SQUARE CO-OP, London.

cards

1 'A blow delivered against British imperialist bourgeois rule by a rebellion in Ireland . . .' (Lenin)
2 'If you remove the English army tomorrow and hoist the green flag over Dublin castle . . .' (Connolly)
3 Self determination for the Irish people. During the guerilla struggle in Northern Ireland, not only the tri-colour flew over the Republican ghettos but alongside it flew the 'Plough and Stars', the flag of Connolly's Citizen Army.
4 Self determination for the Irish people
5 Derry women fight against British imperialism
6 Wherever there is oppression there is resistance
7 'Britain largely based her "brilliant" economic development . . . on the destitution among the Irish peasantry . . .' (Lenin)
8 Support the struggle of Irish prisoners in English jails
9 Support the struggle of the Irish people
10 'The working class will not be free until Ireland is liberated from English oppression . . .' (Marx)
11 Political Status for Irish prisoners
12 Criminalisation of struggle needs normalisation of repression
13 Since imperialism is trying simultaneously to dominate the working class and smother the national liberation struggle . . . then there is only one enemy whom we are fighting
14 The reason why we have young men being tortured daily in the H. Blocks . . .

15 1916: the Easter rising in Dublin
   1969: the rising in the North
16 Irish women fight against British imperialism

'TOWN TOPICS',
30 Chichester Street, Belfast.

card
 1 The largest Union Jack in the World

ULSTER DEFENCE ASSOCIATION
2a Gawn Street, Newtownards Road, Belfast.

cards (Loyalist Murals in Belfast)

 1 1690
 2 Shankill: No Surrender
 3 Cemented with love
 4 One Faith. One Crown
 5 Untitled

ULSTER LIBERAL PARTY

cards
James Murray; European election, n.d.
Rodney Smith; Stormont election, 18 June 1970

ULSTER LOYALIST
DEMOCRATIC PARTY

cards
Billy Elliot; Belfast City Council election, 27 August 1981
John McMichael; Belfast City Council election, 27 August, 1981

ULSTER PUBLISHING CO.,
36 Shankill Road, Belfast.

cards
 1 Tax Collector John and Sir Edward (card 135)
 2 The Ulster seat
 3 The Red Hand of Ulster
 4 The Home Rule Mud Scow
 5 Ulster
 6 West Belfast, Devlin's reserve voters (card 136)
 7 Our artist's dreams of West Belfast sub-tenancy

 8 The Ulster Gun Runners
 9 Gough the brave
10 The Political Alphabet
11 Saviours of Ulster
12 The Home Rule Rout (card 121)
13 Ulster's Covenant
14 Our freedom
15 Cock of the North
16 Who said Home Rule
17 Sir Edward Carson's Bulldog 'Ulster' (card 120)

ULSTER UNIONIST PARTY

cards
Herron; Assembly election, 1982
Martin Smith; Westminster election, 4 March 1982
Stanley McMaster; Westminster election, 10 October 1974
Martin Smyth; Westminster election, 9 June 1983

ULSTER VOLUNTEER FORCE,
Old Town Hall, Belfast.

card
 1 Charge of the Ulster Division (see card 5)

UNIONIST ANTI-WHITE PAPER

card
Michael Brooks; 28 June 1973

UNIONIST PARTY OF
NORTHERN IRELAND

cards
Victor Brennan; Belfast City Council election, 20 May 1982
Eddie Cummings; EEC election, 7 June 1979
Victor Brennan; Westminster election, 3 May 1979
Norman Agnew; Westminster election, 3 May 1979
Anne Dickson; Westminster election, 3 May 1979

UNITED LOYALIST FRONT

card
P. G. Moles / Gerald McVeigh / Jack Scott / Jim Scott; 30 May 1973

UNITED ULSTER UNIONIST PARTY

cards

Robert Gabbey; Assembly election, 20 October 1982

Reg Empty / Ben Horan; Assembly election, 20 October 1982

VALENTINE & SONS,
Dublin and Dundee.

cards

1   Londonderry under Home Rule
2   Belfast makes history
3   Ulster citizen army – Surrender – Never!
4   Shall we have the breath to boom again?
5   We will cross the Boyne again
6   'Bravo Ulster'. Gunrunning in Ulster. The mystery ship Fanny at Larne
7   'Bravo Ulster'. Gunrunning in Ulster. Discharging the Fanny at Donaghadee.
8   'Bravo Ulster'. Gunrunning in Ulster. Discharging the Fanny at Larne.
9   Going too hot for him. (Anti-Carson)
10 Oh! What a fall there'll be. (Anti-Carson) (card 138)
11 Sir Edward Carson (card 49)
12 You can lead a horse to water (card 118)
13 Heroes of the Union
14 No thoroughfare
15 We won't have Home Rule
16 U.L.S.T.E.R.
17 Carrickfergus Castle under Home Rule
18 Against Home Rule – Hands up
19 The Arms and the Men (card 51)
20 The Red Hand and the winning hand (card 52)
21 King George and Queen Mary opening the Irish Parliament
22 The UVF – A Red Cross contingent
23 Sarsfield surprises the Williamite siege train, 11th August, 1690
24 Statue of William III, Dublin
25 The old 'No Home Rule' Convention Hall, Belfast 1892
26 Touch us if you dare
27 Portadown Market Place under Home Rule (card 42)

VOLUNTEER POLITICAL PARTY

card

Ken Gibson; Assembly election, 20 June 1973

W. & K., London.

card

1   The flag that's braved a thousand years

WALTON, W. E.,
39 and 57 Royal Avenue, Belfast.
Jeweller, stationer and fancy goods dealer.

cards

1   Belfast Strike – A train of motor vans under police escort (card 26)
2   Belfast Strike – Motor vans delivering under police escort (card 37)
3   Belfast Strike – Cases of machinery burned near Albert Memorial (card 27)
4   Belfast Strike – Overturned lorries, Gt. George's Street (card 38)
5   Belfast Strike – Overturned lorries near dock (card 28)
6   Men of Workman and Clark's and the North East Unionist Club
7   The Great Ulster Unionist Demonstration, 9th April, 1912
8   The March Past: Ulster Unionist Demonstration, 9th April, 1912
9   Head of procession approaching the Grand Stand, 9th April, 1912
10 Bonar Law, Walter Long etc. watching march past, 9th April, 1912
11 The residence of Capt. James Craig
12 The Windsor and Stranmillis Unionist Club, Belfast. Parading on April 9th, for the Great Demonstration at Balmoral. Headed by Robert Thompson, Esq., D.L., M.P.
13 The Great Ulster Unionist Demonstration, Balmoral Show Grounds, April 9, 1912. Sir Edward Carson putting the resolution – 'Never under any circumstances will we submit to Home Rule'.
14 The Great Unionist Demonstration, April 9th, 1912. Unionist Clubs and Orangemen marching in column, sixteen abreast, past saluting base (the decorated stand in distance): took three hours to file past (card 54)
15 The Great Unionist Demonstration at Ulster Hall, Belfast, on eve of Covenant Day (Sept. 27th, 1912). General view of platform.

16 The Great Unionist Demonstration at Ulster Hall, Belfast, on the eve of Covenant Day (Sept. 27th 1912). The overflow meeting at front of Hall in Bedford Street.

17 The Great Unionist Demonstration at Ulster Hall, Belfast, on eve of Covenant Day 27th Dec. 1912. (General view of body of the Hall)

18 A picked guard of Honour

19 Ulster Covenant Day, Belfast Sept. 28th

1912. The double procession entering the City Hall to sign the Covenant.

20 Ulster Day, Sept. 28th, 1912. Orangemen and Unionist Clubs marching to the City Hall, Belfast to sign the Covenant against Home Rule.

WOOLSTONE BROS., London E.C.

card

1 The Home Ruler

APPENDIX C
THE POSTCARD HAND CAMERA

The letter reproduced here is taken from the New Photographic Catalogue published by Hobbies Limited. The catalogue states:

> There is little need to emphasise the widespread popularity which the Picture Postcard has secured in this country. Every amateur photographer will naturally wish to be in a position to provide his own Pictorial cards, and to make this task easy we are this season introducing a particularly fine series of cameras for taking pictures on plates, of the regulation postcard size. Our postcard Hand Cameras, which constitute the chief novelty of this new catalogue are offered at prices which should induce every amateur photographer to take up this new and exceptionally fascinating branch of work.

By 1904, therefore, the ability to manufacture one's own picture postcards was afforded to the public at large. That many took advantage of this is demonstrated by the large number of such cards, depicting family groups, street scenes, natural disasters etc., which have come down to us. Events such as street riots were eagerly seized upon by these amateur postcard manufacturers and collections of these cards now form important social archives.

Telephone Nº 1353, HOLBORN.

PHOTOGRAPHIC DEPARTMENT.

HOBBIES
Every Saturday
One Penny.

12, Paternoster Square,
LONDON, E.C.

March, 1904.

SPECIAL OFFER.

Dear Sir,

Enclosed we have pleasure in sending you a copy of our
new Photographic Catalogue. We specially invite your attention
to our series of Post Card Cameras, by means of which any
amateur photographer can produce his own pictorial post cards.

We are holding a Great Stocktaking Sale of Fretwork
Tools and Materials, which is to last for three weeks from
March 26th. Photographic goods are not included in this Sale.
To you, however, as one of our regular customers, we shall be
pleased to make a special personal concession. We will allow
you a discount of 1½d. in the shilling on any Cameras or
Photographic Accessories—excepting Kodak goods or Midg Cameras—
providing your order is written on the enclosed form and sent
to us before the conclusion of our Fretwork Sale on April 16th.
We hope you will be able to take advantage of our offer.

Yours faithfully,

HOBBIES LIMITED.

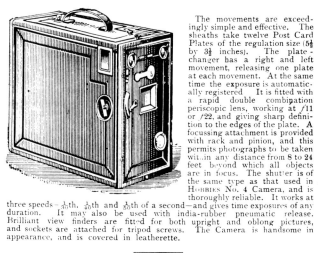

APPENDIX D
THE REPUBLIC

On 13 December 1906 there appeared on the streets of Belfast an ambitious but short-lived newspaper called *The Republic*. Its editor was Bulmer Hobson, founder member of the Dungannon Club whose ideal of national independence for Ireland it propounded. Its offices were at 114 Royal Avenue, Belfast. At this time such a paper had a better chance of fulfilling its propaganda aims in a provincial town rather than in the capital, Dublin. In a short article in the first issue of *The Republic*, Hobson stated:

> We stand for an Irish Republic because we see no compromise with England, no repeal of the Union, no concession of Home Rule, or Devolution will satisfy the national aspirations of the Irish people nor allow the unrestricted mental, moral and material development of the country. National independence is our right; we ask no more and we will accept no less.

The teaching of Wolfe Tone and John O'Leary greatly influenced Hobson throughout his life and those articles in *The Republic* contributed by him bear testimony to this. Complete separation from England, a united people working for the good of the whole nation, and a policy of passive resistance to English authority were the watchwords of *The Republic*.

Throughout its short life money was lacking to run the newspaper successfully. It was set up with the aid of £60 borrowed from various friends, and at no time were contributors paid. Contributors, other than Hobson

himself, included J. W. Good, then a journalist on the conservative *Northern Whig* newspaper, Robert Lynd, the essayist and enthusiastic member of the London Gaelic League, P. S. O'Hegarty, author of numerous books of Irish history, John P. Campbell, brother of the poet Joseph Campbell and illustrator of Irish texts, and the three Morrow brothers, George, Jack and Norman, members of an artistic and literary Belfast family much involved in the cultural life of their native city. The articles contributed by these men were usually short, to the point, and unambiguous. Each issue contained a full-page cartoon attacking British army recruitment in Ireland, nationalist involvement at Westminster, or any proposed form of diluted independence such as that offered by the devolution bill; later, cartoons were used to extol the vigorous self-help principles of the newly founded Sinn Féin movement. In every issue of *The Republic* sets of nationalist postcards were advertised for sale and it is from these advertisements that much of our information concerning the Dungannon Club postcards is gleaned.

The political cartoons, drawn by Lynd, Campbell or one of the Morrow brothers, were black-and-white, unambiguously nationalist and visually striking. As early as the second issue of *The Republic*, 20 December 1906, the idea of reproducing them as postcards had matured to the extent that an advertisement for them appeared on the inside back cover. Ten cartoons were reproduced as postcards. In addition three other cards were advertised, two of which depict scenes relating to the northern United Irishmen, the third being a portrait of the dead Fenian, John O'Leary. We are fortunate in that we are able to date the publication of these postcards very exactly. Below is a list of the cards with the date on which they first appeared in *The Republic* as a cartoon and the date when they were first advertised as postcards.

TITLE OF POSTCARD

1. The Battle of Antrim (card 15)
2. The Old Chapel of St. Mary, Belfast
3. Catching Recruits (card 10)
4. The Stranger in the House (card 17)
5. The Secret of England's Greatness
6. Sinn Féin and Prosperity (card 21)
7. The Wild Geese, 1907
8. Devolution Pie (card 19)
9. Ulster: The Parting of the Ways
10. John Bull's Famous Circus (card 20)
11. Portrait of the Dead Fenian, John O'Leary
12. Irish Anti-National Exhibition
13. John Bull and Sinn Féin

DATE OF PUBLICATION AS CARTOON IN THE REPUBLIC

1	Vol. 1 No. 1	13 December 1906
2	Vol. 1 No. 1	13 December 1906
3	Vol. 1 No. 2	20 December 1906
4	Vol. 1 No. 3	27 December 1906
5	Vol. 1 No. 6	17 January 1907
6	Vol. 1 No. 7	24 January 1907
7	Vol. 1 No. 11	21 February 1907
8	Vol. 1 No. 12	28 February 1907
9	Vol. 1 No. 13	7 March 1907
10	Vol. 1 No. 15	21 March 1907
11	This card did not appear as a cartoon.	
12	Vol. 1 No. 16	28 March 1907
13	Vol. 1 No. 18	11 April 1907

DATE OF ADVERTISEMENT AS POSTCARD

1	13 December 1906	7	11 April 1907
2	13 December 1906	8	11 April 1907
3	20 December 1906	9	11 April 1907
4	27 December 1906	10	11 April 1907
5	11 April 1907	12	11 April 1907
6	11 April 1907	13	11 April 1907

In all, twenty-six issues of *The Republic* were published before lack of funds and Hobson's transfer to Dublin occasioned its demise. It aimed at, and was content with, that central aim of its propaganda, the creation of a confident and unbreakable republican spirit among its readers.

APPENDIX E

THE EASTER REBELLION, 1916

When the European war broke out in August 1914, both Carson and Redmond pledged their complete support for the British government's war effort. As a compromise measure the Home Rule bill passed onto the statute book, but its implementation was postponed until hostilities ceased. The leaders of the opposing camps in Ireland fully expected to be rewarded for their loyalty by the achievement of their political demands.

But, although the bulk of the National Volunteers were totally in agreement with Redmond's policy and many rushed to join the British army, there was also a sizeable minority who saw the coming war as the ideal opportunity to break England's domination of Ireland once and for all. This group, under Eoin MacNeill, seceded from the National Volunteers in September 1914 to form the Irish Volunteers, and it was from this group that the leaders of the rebellion were to come.

Even within the newly formed Irish Volunteers there was a difference of opinion as to the best means of achieving Ireland's independence. Eoin MacNeill and Bulmer Hobson were in favour of a cautious and circumspect policy, relying on international negotiations at the end of the war to solve the country's nationality question. James Connolly, Patrick Pearse, Thomas Clarke and Arthur Griffith (139) were convinced that the time was quickly coming when an armed insurrection would overthrow the English presence in Ireland for ever, and establish the government of Ireland in the hands of the Irish. They pursued their secret aims mainly through the Irish Republican Brotherhood (IRB), but their need to deceive MacNeill and Hobson led ultimately to confusion and the eventual countermanding of the order to the National Volunteers to take up arms.

The date for the insurrection was set for 23 April 1916 (Easter Sunday) but MacNeill found out and issued orders cancelling armed hostilities. Connolly, Pearse, Clarke and Griffith were determined to launch the insurrection and re-scheduled it for the next day, Easter Monday. The confusing and conflicting orders emanating from the leadership of the Irish Volunteers served to prevent a general uprising in the country and to centralise the fighting in Dublin.

At noon on Easter Monday Pearse led his forces into the General Post Office in Sackville Street (now O'Connell Street) and fortified it as best he could against attack. From the steps of the building he read out the Proclamation of the Irish Republic (140), which had been composed by himself, Connolly and Thomas MacDonagh, and printed at Liberty Hall. Inside the GPO all the telegraph wires were cut, thus isolating the city from the rest of the country, but

the failure to seize the Telephone Exchange in Crown Alley cost them dearly. Buildings suitable for fortification and defence were taken over throughout the city and the insurgents settled down to await the inevitable onslaught of the military garrisoned in Dublin.

All through Monday night British army reinforcements were hastily summoned from the Curragh, Belfast and from England, and on Tuesday 25 April these troops began to arrive in the city. They were deployed immediately, and within a very short time the rebels' strongholds were surrounded. Most of the main thoroughfares in central Dublin were impassable and unsuspecting motorists and carters had their vehicles commandeered for barricades (141). Furniture shops were broken into and their contents used to protect the troops (142), but the populace of Dublin had other ideas about the use to which such furniture could be put and looting was widespread throughout the week of fighting.

On Tuesday night, 25 April, martial law was enforced to meet the exigencies of the situation. More troops and artillery continued to pour into Dublin and the populace of the capital saw a strange assortment of hastily constructed armoured vehicles trundling through their streets (143). At eight o'clock on Wednesday morning the admiralty steamer, *Helga,* came up the Liffey and bombarded Liberty Hall, the headquarters of Connolly's Citizen Army (144). Artillery brought from Trinity College into Tara Street was also used to shell the building. By the afternoon of Wednesday the military were in possession of Brunswick Street and all the district between that thoroughfare and the river, and right up to D'Olier Street.

The military authorities placed sentries at the entrance to a lane leading

from D'Olier Street to the Theatre
Royal. The soldiers had not been long
there before one of the snipers in Kelly's
shop at the corner of Bachelor's Walk
shot one of them dead. The military
then brought a nine pounder gun into
position at Trinity College facing
D'Olier Street and bombarded Kelly's
Corner (145).

The fighting reached its climax on
Thursday and Friday. Artillery was
brought into play at every point and the
bombardment continued throughout
the night. The Hotel Metropole and the
block of buildings stretching into
Middle Abbey Street were destroyed by
shell and fire – buildings destroyed
included the offices of the *Freeman's
Journal* and the *Evening Telegraph*. On
the opposite side of Sackville Street, all
the shops were burned down from
Hopkin's Corner at O'Connell Bridge
to the Tramway Company's offices at
Cathedral Street. Also destroyed were
almost all the houses between Eden
Quay and Lower Abbey Street down to
Marlborough Street. The flames from
the Metropole Hotel spread to the
General Post Office and hastened its
evacuation. On Saturday 29 April
Pearse, Connolly and McDonagh were
forced to order an unconditional
surrender.

With barely two thousand at their
command the leaders of the insurrection
had held out against vastly superior
numbers of trained soldiers for a week.
Their achievement, however, was
anything but popular in the immediate
aftermath of their surrender. The
Dublin crowd, through which many of
them were marched to imprisonment,
was hostile and angry. John Redmond
condemned them in the British House
of Parliament and the *Freeman's Journal*
– possibly the most widely-read
contemporary newspaper in Ireland –
denounced their actions. It seemed that
not only had they lost the battle, but

they had lost their cause as well. Within
a fortnight, however, the situation had
drastically and irrevocably changed.

The leaders of the insurrection were
tried under martial law, found guilty of
treason, sentenced to death and
executed almost immediately. Of the
fifteen men who were executed, all
seven who signed the Proclamation died
by firing squad, along with eight others
who had taken a prominent part in the
fighting (146). As the terse announce-
ment of each death issued from official
sources the whole of Ireland seemed
caught up in an unreal world of suspense
and disbelief. By the time James
Connolly and Sean MacDermott were
shot on 12 May 1916, Pearse's blood
sacrifice had been realised and public
opinion had swung into line behind the
separatist ideals of the leaders of the
insurrection.

PUBLISHERS OF 1916 POSTCARDS

BAIRD, W. & G., Belfast (1916)
  1 Ruins Hotel Metropole and Corner of
  GPO

CURRAN PUBLISHERS, Dublin (1916)
  1 Cornelius Colbert
  2 Edward Daly

THE DAILY SKETCH (1916)
  1 Irish Rebellion, May 1916. Sackville
  Street in Flames.
  2 Irish Rebellion, May 1916. Talbot
  Street, Dublin, held against a rebel
  charge.
  3 Irish Rebellion, May 1916. Soldiers
  holding a Dublin street.
  4 Irish Rebellion, May 1916. Ruined
  Sackville Street, Dublin, barricaded
  with motor cars (card 141).
  5 Irish Rebellion, May 1916. Soldiers
  bivouacking opposite Liberty Hall, the
  Rebel Headquarters in Dublin.

6 Irish Rebellion, May 1916. The General Post Office, Dublin (Rebel Headquarters) destroyed.
7 Irish Rebellion, May 1916. Liberty Hall, Dublin, the Rebel Headquarters after the storming.
8 Irish Rebellion, May 1916. The Interior of the Ballroom, Imperial Hotel, Dublin, after the Siege.
9 Irish Rebellion, May 1916. Arrest of Edmund Kent, at 4 a.m.
10 Irish Rebellion, May 1916. Searching a hay-cart for Rebels or ammunition.

HELY'S LTD., Dublin (1916)
1 The Insurrection in Dublin – Armoured Motor Car in Bachelor's Walk.
2 Exterior of GPO after evacuation, showing broken flag-post from which Republican flag was flown.
3 Liberty Hall, Headquarters of the Citizen Army, after Bombardment (card 144).
4 Sackville Street, opposite GPO, showing all that is standing of the Imperial Hotel and Messrs. Clery's Drapery Establishment.
5 Liberty Hall, Headquarters of the Citizen Army, after Bombardment (different from (3) above).
6 After the Insurrection – Linenhall Barracks.
7 After the Insurrection – Sackville Street from Eden Quay to Abbey Street.
8 After the Insurrection – Ruins in Eden Quay.
9 After the Insurrection – Corner of Bachelor's Walk and Lower Sackville Street (card 145).
10 After the Insurrection – Interior General Post Office, Dublin.

IRISH ART PUBLICATIONS LTD., Dublin 1 (1966)
1 1916 Commemoration Souvenir. Casement at Banna Strand.
2 1916 Commemoration Souvenir. The Asgard.
3 1916 Commemoration Souvenir. Padraig Pearse reads the Proclamation.
4 1916 Commemoration Souvenir. The Battle of Carlisle Bridge.

139. Arthur Griffith, first president of Dáil Éireann, was foremost in advocating armed rebellion against the English presence in Ireland. This postcard, published by Keogh Bros., Dublin, was produced after his death in August 1922.

5 1916 Commemoration Souvenir. Inside the General Post Office.
6 1916 Commemoration Souvenir. The Destruction of Liberty Hall.
7 1916 Commemoration Souvenir. Sackville Street after the Conflict.
8 1916 Commemoration Souvenir. The First Dáil.
9 1916 Commemoration Souvenir. Beggar's Bush.
10 1916 Commemoration Souvenir. John F. Kennedy at Arbour Hill.
11 1916 Commemoration Souvenir. Pádraig Mac Piarais.

THE PROCLAMATION OF
POBLACHT NA H EIREANN.
THE PROVISIONAL GOVERNMENT
OF THE
IRISH REPUBLIC
TO THE PEOPLE OF IRELAND.

IRISHMEN AND IRISHWOMEN: In the name of God and of the dead generations
o m which she receives her old tradition of nationhood, Ireland, through us, summons
r children to her flag and strikes for her freedom.

Having organised and trained her manhood through her secret revolutionary
ganisation, the Irish Republican Brotherhood, and through her open military
rganisations, the Irish Volunteers and the Irish Citizen Army, having patiently
rfected her discipline, having resolutely waited for the right moment to reveal
elf, she now seizes that moment, and, supported by her exiled children in America
nd by gallant allies in Europe, but relying in the first on her own strength, j
rikes in full confidence of victory.

We decla   t of the people of Ireland to the ownership of Ireland, and
e unfettered   Irish destinies, to be sover   and indefeasible.   The lo
urpation of th   by a foreign people and government has not extinguished t
ght, nor can it e   tinguished exce   he destruction of the Irish people.
 very generation   e ha   ted their right to national freedom a
vereignty;   ree hundred years they have asser
ms. Stan   al right a   again asserting it i
the wor   Irish R
d We r
its w

shm
ghts
o.

An CHAISC 1916

141. Below - Motorcars, carts, furniture and any other available cover were used to form barricades. This postcard produced by *The Daily Sketch* shows the after effects of the fighting on such temporary barricades.

140. Left - The Proclamation of the Irish Republic is a very revered and emotive document in nationalist circles. It is used as the backdrop in this postcard, published by the Republican movement to commemorate the men of 1916.

Irish Rebellion May 1916
Ruined Sackville Street Dublin barricaded with Motor Cars

Irish Rebellion. May 1916.
Soldiers holding a Dublin Street.

142. The military was also adept at building improvised barricades. This postcard, published by *The Daily Sketch*, shows such a barricade.

KEOGH BROS., Dublin (1916)
1 Sean McDermott (card 146)
2 Arthur Griffith T.D. (CARD 139)

THE REPUBLICAN MOVEMENT
(1916)
1 The Proclamation of Poblacht na h-Éireann (card 140)

ROTARY PHOTOGRAPHIC SERIES
(1916)
1 The Sinn Féin Revolt in Dublin. The Ruins of Liberty Hall.

The Insurrection in Dublin.—Armoured Motor Car in Bachelor's Walk.

Liberty Hall, Headquarters of the Citizen Army, after Bombardment.

After the Insurrection.—
Corner of Bachelor's Walk and Lr. Sackville Street
which commanded O'Connell Bridge.

145. Above - The premises of Kelly & Son were bombarded and much damage was done to them after a military sentry had been killed by sniper fire there. This postcard, published by Hely's Ltd., Dublin,, shows the extent of the damage.

143. Opposite top - Technical ingenuity was used to produce some very strange looking vehicles. This postcard, published by Hely's Ltd., Dublin, shows a heavily armoured truck with rifle holes along front and side.

144. Left - Liberty Hall, headquarters of Connolly's citizen army, was shelled by the '*Helga*' and by artillery brought from Trinity College.

Sean McDermott

146. Sean MacDermott was executed by firing squad on 12 May 1916. He had been inducted into the Irish Republican Brotherhood by Bulmer Hobson and Denis McCullough in 1906, but favoured the 'physical force' methods of Pearse and Connolly.

VALENTINE, Dublin (1916)

1 Sinn Féin Rebellion. Hotel Metropole and Post Office, Dublin. Before and after.
2 Sinn Féin Rebellion. Sackville Street, Dublin. Before and after.
3 Sinn Féin Rebellion. DBC Sackville Street, Dublin.
4 Sinn Féin Rebellion, 1916. Sackville Street, Dublin.
5 Sinn Féin Rebellion, 1916. Smoking Ruins on the side of the Liffey, Dublin.
6 Sinn Féin Rebellion, 1916. Inside the General Post Office, Dublin.
7 Sinn Féin Rebellion, 1916. DBC Sackville Street, Dublin (different from (3) above).
8 Sinn Féin Rebellion 1916. Corner of Sackville Street, Dublin.
9 Sinn Féin Rebellion, 1916. Hotel Metropole and Post Office, Dublin.
10 Sinn Féin Rebellion, 1916. Wrecked shops in Sackville Street, Dublin.
11 Sinn Féin Rebellion, 1916. Liberty Hall, Dublin.
12 The Quays from O'Connell Bridge, Dublin. (After the Rebellion.)

APPENDIX F

POSTCARD VALUES

Postcard collecting has blossomed so much in the past decade that enthusiasts need to have some idea of the cost of starting and adding to their collections. However, the prices of cards differ from area to area and from dealer to dealer, so it is possibly more helpful to speak of a card's 'rarity'. Political cards can vary in price from £1 to £10 and upwards depending on the content of the card. Of the postcards illustrated in this book, the cheapest and easiest to acquire are the modern cards: party political election postcards arrive free through our letterboxes; modern propaganda cards sell for around 10 pence apiece and can be bought from some of the firms mentioned in Appendix B. The next in the 'rarity' scale are the 1907 strike cards. These are quite difficult to trace and will cost from £1.50 upwards. The anti-Home Rule cards are much sought after and highly prized. They range in price from £2 to £10 and higher. I have not seen a 1906/7 Sinn Féin card offered for sale, and feel that their existence is not widely known in the postcard world. Their rarity will undoubtedly increase their monetary value with single cards selling for £5 and upwards. It should be stressed that there is no fixed price for postcards; collectors must make up their own minds concerning the price they are prepared to pay for a card, using their own criteria of value.